THE LIVING TABLE

RECIPES AND DEVOTIONS
FOR EVERYDAY GET-TOGETHERS

ABBY TURNER

DaySpring
LIVE YOUR FAITH

The Living Table: Recipes and Devotions for Everyday Get-Togethers
Copyright © 2021 Abby Turner. All rights reserved.
First Edition, March 2021

Published by:

21154 Highway 16 East
Siloam Springs, AR 72761
dayspring.com

Written by: Abby Turner
Cover/Inside Photography: Molly Anne Sandefur
Prop/Food Stylist: Abby Turner
Design by: Becca Barnett

Printed in China
Prime: J3112
ISBN: 978-1-64454-849-3

TABLE OF CONTENTS

INTRODUCTION

Writing this cookbook has been a labor of love. You see, I'm not a writer by trade. If I had it my way, we would be sitting around my table drinking coffee with peppermint mocha creamer and nomming on chocolate chip cookies. Instead, here we are. I'm sitting on my couch with my two adorable papillon puppies typing away as fast as my little fingers can type. Before we dive into easy recipes, party themes, and building community, I want to share a little bit about who I am and where I come from.

Born and raised in Arkansas, I'm as Southern as a girl can get. If my two sisters and I weren't at school, we were at church, and if we weren't at church, we were sitting around the table eating together. The table—it's where I grew up, the place where I laughed, cried, shared exciting news (and not so exciting news), debated with my sisters, and opened my heart to Jesus. I didn't realize how much that table meant to me until I moved away.

At age twenty-four, I moved to Birmingham, Alabama. For the first time in my life I lived alone and worked long hours, leaving little time for community and friendships. Lonely and depressed, I thought my life was incomplete because I was single. I threw myself at dating apps and constantly felt discouraged. After weeks of hearing me complain about my terrible life, my mom offered me the best advice I've ever received: "God calls us to serve people. Why don't you cook a meal and invite people over?" And then she finished with a phrase that she has repeated over the years to my sisters and me: "Be a blessing."

After rolling my eyes and grumbling for longer than I would like to admit, I took my mother's advice. I cracked open a cookbook and hosted dinner for friends for the first time in my adult life. The four of us squeezed around a table for two—and had the best time. I will always remember that night because I made four-cheese tortellini. It was terrible. But that night God taught me something important: I was lonely, not because I was single, but because I had not been investing in and nurturing a community in my life.

That night Jesus ignited in me a desire for

community, a realization of the importance of the table, and a curiosity for the art of hospitality. Fast-forward seven years and here we are.

I didn't go to culinary school or watch a ton of YouTube videos to learn to cook. I learned by trial and error with my community as my test kitchen. Cooking for me is therapeutic and helps me bond with people. The kitchen is my happy place, but it wasn't always that way. Being comfortable in the kitchen was a discipline—a muscle—I learned to love.

After four years of cooking for friends and hosting dinner parties every week (around my very small apartment table), I decided to share my love of hospitality with the world and launched my blog, A Table Top Affair. I also started posting my recipes and party ideas on Pinterest and Instagram. I wanted to encourage people who were stuck in a rut, people who didn't know how to meet others or how to cultivate their own community. So I began trying to put a formula to it—a formula for empowering people to overcome their insecurities in the kitchen and to truly invest in opening their homes even though they might not have the picture-perfect family.

It took me being single and lonely to see that God had big plans for me around my kitchen table. If I wasn't single or had put off embracing hospitality until I had a husband and 2.5 kids, I would have missed all the memories, relationships, and conversations about Jesus around that table.

The table is important—that piece of wood or metal or plastic that sits about forty-two inches high and some of us eat at. For some of you that table holds bills, the laundry, and kid's soccer shoes. Sadly, not much eating happens there these days. The majority of us eat on the go. And many homes these days are removing the table altogether and building in bars with stools.

We have traded our tables for sofas and seventy-inch TVs, removed our dining rooms and turned them into game rooms, and ignored the most important piece of furniture in the entire home.

In Exodus, after God brings the Israelites out of Egypt and they arrive at Mount Sinai, He gives them the Ten Commandments. Following those commands, God provides instructions on building the tabernacle. In Exodus 25, He starts with building the ark of the covenant followed by the building of the table. There is no mistaking the significance of the table.

After reading Exodus 25 I immediately thought, *Wow! My God wants me first to worship Him and then second, to dine with Him at the table.* In Exodus 25:30 God tells Moses, "Place the Bread of the Presence on the table to remain before Me at all times" (NLT). I can't help but think that the Bread of the Presence is exactly what Jesus refers to as the "bread of life" in John 6:35, when He says, "I am the bread of life. Whoever comes to Me will never be hungry again. Whoever believes in Me will never be thirsty" (NLT). Let's take this a step further: God wants to be at the table with us every single time we sit there. I believe that's what He was saying in Exodus 25:30 when He was talking to Moses. He was asking us to sit at the table with Him, commune with Him, and enter into His peace. God, in His infinite wisdom, designed the table to be a safe place where the human soul receives healing from past events, forgiveness from past actions, and a deep-seated love that only comes from the presence of God.

At some deep level, I believe we are drawn to the table. When Jesus said, "I am the bread of life," I believe He literally meant for us to bring people to the table and serve them, and to let Him do the rest. When we set the table and prepare a meal, there is something supernatural that happens to our hearts. It's undeniable!

Throughout this book, it is my hope that you will be inspired to clean off your table and prepare to serve others. In fact, I have an easy go-to handbook that is full of tips on how to be prepared to serve. Trust me, I know life gets overwhelming and busy, but God longs for us to release all our pressures to Him. He wants us to live peaceful lives—lives that are full of joy and fellowship.

It is so important that we don't lose sight of the significance of hospitality amid the busyness of life in today's world. And it's crucial that we don't lose sight of God's desire for us to live in community—His desire for us to have deep, meaningful relationships in which we support and pray and care for one another. When we make the time and effort to practice hospitality—to intentionally gather around the table with people—we build a strong community that spurs "one another on toward love and good deeds" (Hebrews 10:24 NIV).

The table is the first piece of furniture (after the ark of the covenant) God instructs the Israelites to make for the tabernacle—the place where He would meet with His people—and it's the last piece of furniture Jesus sat at before He died. Let that sink in. The table literally bookends God's love story to us in addition to being laced throughout Scripture. There is absolutely no question about it: the table is important.

Because the table—and what it represents—is so meaningful, I've devoted much of my time and energy to learning how to cultivate a heart that seeks to give to others around my table in the form of hospitality. It's something I've had to work at. I've also had to work hard at accepting that I'm single—not because I want to be, but because that's just where I'm at right now. I haven't dated in years, and honestly, the horizon looks pretty bleak. So I've been working through the concept of being hospitable while being single for a while now. I have done a ton of research on this. (I must admit, my research is partly motivated by me trying to find some supernatural prayer I can pray so I don't have to be single.) Everything I have read and studied has pointed me to community and to Christ. You and I were designed by God with souls that crave Him, and nothing else can fill that craving but living for Him. No date, no marriage, no man can satisfy us like God can.

It's easy to believe the lie that hospitality can only happen when you have a home, a husband, 2.5 kids, and a dog. As it turns out, the two women in Scripture who always get brought up when discussing hospitality are Mary and Martha. These two ladies demonstrate two of the most important disciplines of hospitality: the keeper of the home (Martha) and the encourager and communicator (Mary). And guess what? Theologians believe they were single!

What about you? Have you thought about opening your home, cooking, preparing for people to visit? Maybe you don't have a home with a table or maybe your hospitality looks like getting people together for a potluck, or at the coffee shop around a coffee table, or around a table at a local restaurant. What does practicing hospitality mean to you?

When God revealed the importance of the table to me, I knew I had to act. I was amazed at the support and encouragement from those who sat around my own two-top table, and I wanted others to have the same experience. However, I quickly learned that people were intimidated by the kitchen, insecure about hosting, and did not feel confident when it came to inviting people into their home. That is when I started my blog, A Table Top Affair.

With my blog I strive to bring people to the table—not just to my table, but to yours too. My recipes are easy and quick. You see, I learned very early on that hosting does not require food that takes all day to prepare. It's not about being perfect; it's about offering "hospitality to one another without grumbling" (I Peter 4:9 NIV). So, my recipes are geared toward the busy professional, the working mom, the stay-at-home mother of three. I look at recipes through the lens of one pot, thirty minutes, easy cleanup.

No matter what phase of life you are in (single, married, mom with littles, empty nester, or recently retired), loneliness can overwhelm any one of us. It's our community that encourages us through the ups and downs of our lives, and through this interaction we get to experience the joy of God's goodness. So, what do you think? Is God calling you to dust off your table and open your door? If so, why not follow His lead? After all, He will be with you throughout the process, giving you everything you need.

And I'll be with you, too. I want you to treat this book as your friend. Keep it close and let it help you bring people into your home and around your table.

I hope the recipes encourage you. I hope they provide inspiration for ways to be hospitable, parties to host, or food to take to friends in need. Most importantly, I hope they bring people to your table because—and speaking from experience—when people gather around a table, God seems to move in crazy, big ways.

Let's be real. I mess up food a lot, but the goal is to glorify God at the table with old and new friends while my two adorable papillon puppies beg for scraps at the foot of the table.

My prayer is that the joy of hospitality that permeates the pages of this book will begin to infect your life.

Dear God,

I pray over this book and over the people who read it. I pray that You give us eyes to see the needs of people. Help us understand what it means to love others as we love ourselves. God, only You can teach us to care for those who are sick and to have empathy for strangers. May You fill our hearts with generosity to invite others over and the strength to smile and lend a helping hand when the opportunity presents itself. Lord, only You can fill the God-sized hole in each of our souls. In Jesus's name, I pray. Amen.

HOW TO USE THIS BOOK

One of the most repeated statements I hear is "I just don't know what to make." The traditional cookbook has recipes distributed by course. You, as the preparer, must decide which recipes to pair together. Then you must calculate prep time and cook time to ensure everything is ready on time.

This is when confusion starts to set in. You become overwhelmed and, in most cases, give up.

Like I mentioned in the Introduction, the table is an important part of life. We should begin thinking of how we can integrate the table into every moment of our lives. I've distributed my recipes by everyday moments. Every recipe can stand alone for each occasion and needs no additional pairing. The majority of the recipes take between thirty minutes and an hour—and they are all dummy-proof.

Each chapter starts off with an inspirational devotion and a few Food for Thought self-reflection questions. These questions are meant to stretch you, encourage you to reflect on what God is trying to teach you, and help you consider how to integrate a hospitality-first mentality into your own life. My prayer is that through this cookbook we begin to change the mindset of an entire generation of people who are intimidated to host and struggle to cultivate deep, God-centered friendships.

Each section of this book is categorized by a different way Christ teaches us to serve others. I chose to divide it this way because whether we realize it or not, we live life through the little moments that help build our relationships with people. Each "table" provides inspiration around ways you can serve others. Some are as small as a Coffee Date, while others are larger get-togethers like Friendsgiving. When we can identify those moments, we can begin to intentionally serve others with food and invite them in to have meaningful conversations that cultivate deep, God-centered friendships.

The Table That Connects grounds us in ways we can build relationships with others. God didn't intend for us to be alone, and connection is the first step in surrounding yourself with a solid tribe of people.

The Table That Teaches is meant to inspire you with ways to bring people to your table and ideas for what to cook when you are teaching others at church, in prayer group, or in your community group at your home.

The Table That Parties represents those moments in life when you are simply having fun with others. Food becomes a catalyst for having a party, enjoying being part of a group of people, and growing deeper in your friendships.

The Table That Serves in Scripture is the table that Jesus calls us to sit at during vulnerable moments of life when people in our community need authentic, deep-rooted love.

The Table That Celebrates is the one we sit around during joyous times of the year. These can be small or large get-togethers, but we can't celebrate life's moments without the holidays, right?

The Table That Welcomes is the table that sets the tone for all the get-togethers. It's the open-armed love of God that encourages and—most importantly—welcomes all types of people.

BEING PREPARED

For by grace you have been saved through faith. And this is not your own doing; it is the gift of God, not a result of works, so that no one may boast. For we are his workmanship, created in Christ Jesus for good works, which God prepared beforehand, that we should walk in them (Ephesians 2:8–10 ESV).

During some seasons of life it can be difficult to imagine that God wants to use us to share His love with other people. Sometimes we struggle with doubt or hopelessness, or we write ourselves off as too sinful or too selfish for God to use (I know that last one resonates with me). God doesn't want us to just go through the motions. He wants us to glorify Him. As the apostle Paul says in Ephesians 2:10, we were created in Christ to do good works. You won't find true satisfaction or fulfillment in anything that doesn't point all glory back to Him. That means that if you spend your life working to be more successful, to be more appreciated, maybe even be more loved in the world's eyes, you will be running on a treadmill—going nowhere. But if you allow God to use you to love and serve others, you will be filled with the fullness of life. To point all glory back to God, we must do our part and be prepared. We need to take time in prayer, spend time in His Word, and be in community with His people so we can encourage one another.

Just like we must be prepared (through prayer and His Word) in our spiritual life to encourage

and lift up one another, we must be prepared in our physical life to serve others. So let's start with the kitchen! In the next few pages, you'll learn how to prepare (and stay prepared) for last-minute meals and get-togethers.

Keep in mind—you won't become an expert overnight! However, I guarantee if you start here and begin practicing the discipline of hospitality, you will get closer to expert status. Even better than that, you'll come away prepared to serve others in your home. And (hopefully) you'll even start inviting people over!

SETTING THE TABLE

It's not about being perfect; it's about being present. And in order to have people around your table, your table must be set. So remove the bills and the laundry, wipe off the dust, and let's get started. It's not hard. I choose to be approachable. I choose to be simple. I have learned that the less formal a seated gathering is, the more open people will be. Their guard comes down and they become vulnerable. And it's when we are vulnerable at the table that we can begin to build deep, meaningful relationships—ones that are truly rooted in God's heart for us. So here are a few options for setting the table.

- Colorful serving pieces are fun, but white goes with every season and makes the food pop!

- Start collecting wooden boards. They are fun and versatile and can be used in plating, serving, and prepping.

- Small bowls ranging from ¼ cup size to 1 cup size are perfect for appetizers, dips, desserts, and more. These can be really colorful and fun!

- Large spoons and forks can add a lot of personality to your serving line or food dishes on the table.

PRO TIP:
Collect an assortment of serving pieces.

KNOWING YOUR GUESTS

Wouldn't it be great if we could all feed five thousand people like Jesus did (Matthew 14:13–21)? Feeding that many people would break most of our budgets. The next few pages contain estimates of what to prepare so you can gauge how much you need and make sure your guests leave happy and not hungry—or thirsty.

How much will they eat and drink? You know your friends, so adjust as necessary. Note: Do not feel obligated to serve everything listed below. When you have people over, they are usually just thankful that you have something for them to eat.

These estimates are based on a three-hour formal party you might throw (think bridal showers, dinner parties, etc.).

ICE: 1 pound per person

SODAS: 3 per person

HORS D'OEUVRES

- Strive for 3–4 different nibbles before a dinner.

- Try to include different types of ingredients, textures, and colors to add some personality to the table.

BASIC APPS: 1–2 appetizers (2–3 bites per guest) when your friends arrive, 30 minutes before dinner

4:00–6:00 P.M. OR 8:00–10:00 P.M.: 2–3 appetizers (4–6 bites per guest) when your friends are hanging out for 2 hours and you aren't serving dinner

6:00–8:00 P.M.: 3–4 appetizers (6–8 bites per guest) when you are having friends over during "dinner time" but not serving a dinner

WHEN APPETIZERS *ARE* THE MEAL: 4–6 appetizers (8–10 bites per guest) when you are having friends over and planning on grazing the entire time

MAIN DISHES

- When I make dinner for friends I try to always include a protein, two greens (usually a salad and a veggie), and a bread.

- I always include bread, even if I have corn or potatoes (but you don't have to).

PROTEIN: 6–8 ounces per guest

VEGETABLES: 3½ ounces per guest

STARCH (CORN, POTATOES, BREAD, ETC.): 5 ounces per guest

RICE AND GRAINS: 1½ to 2 ounces per guest as a side dish. If making risotto as the main course, you need 3 ounces per guest.

PASTA: 2 ounces per guest for a side dish and 4 ounces per guest as a main dish

GREEN SALAD: 1 ounce per guest

DESSERTS

- 2–3 bite-size desserts, cookies, or nibbles per guest

- When cutting a cake or pie, cut a 2-inch wedge per guest

- 4–5 ounces of a creamy dessert like pudding or ice cream per guest

PANTRY STAPLES

When I grocery shop with a hospitality-first mindset, my goal is to keep my kitchen and pantry stocked with certain staples and essentials.

What is a hospitality-first mindset? It is the mindset in which you put serving others first. Ask yourself this question: What moments could happen this week where I need to serve others? Dinner? Bible study? Girls Night? Will I have an unexpected guest and need breakfast for them?

All those thoughts cross my mind when I look into my fridge and pantry. If someone comes into my home this week, what will I need so I'm fully prepared to serve them well?

DINNER FOR FRIENDS

- Fresh or frozen vegetables—I love the pre-cut fresh veggies that come sealed in the produce section.

- Chicken—I always keep fresh chicken breasts in my fridge. If my friends won't eat them, I will.

- Pasta—I always have spaghetti, risotto, fresh refrigerated ravioli, and pappardelle (my favorite).

- Gourmet pizza—there are some really great inexpensive frozen pizzas that have fresh and trendy ingredients like goat cheese, spinach, mushrooms, and roasted veggies. You can even find wood-fired frozen pizzas too!

- Salad—always keep the fixings for salads:
  - Baby arugula
  - Spinach
  - Pecans, pistachios, walnuts
  - Strawberries
  - Goat cheese
- Salad dressings

- Artisan boxed mac 'n' cheese—Gouda, white cheddar, and Havarti are my go-to flavors when searching for specialty cheeses. (Yes! I keep boxed mac 'n' cheese in my pantry at all times; it's a great go-to side dish.)

THROW-AND-GO APPETIZERS FOR LAST-MINUTE GET-TOGETHERS

- Fresh veggies and French onion dip

- My white queso is an easy appetizer and just needs tortilla chips and Velveeta Queso Blanco, white American cheese, heavy cream, and Ro-Tel.

- Marinated olives—I marinate green and black olives with olive oil and an everyday seasoning that includes onion and garlic powder. They are amazing.

- Frozen appetizer staples:
  - Fried goat cheese balls—serve with drizzled honey
  - Spinach and mushroom puff pastries—serve with ranch dip
  - Boneless chicken bites—serve with BBQ sauce or ranch dip
  - Spanakopitas and samosas are always great options too!

BREAKFAST FOR AN UNEXPECTED GUEST

- Veggie and egg hash—frozen veggies, frozen hash browns, eggs, and cheese (super easy!)

- Cinnamon rolls

- Powdered donuts

- Fresh fruit—I try to have at least 2–3 fruits in my house at a time.

- Crescent rolls with breakfast sausage and cream cheese (I keep those three ingredients in my fridge at all times).

PRO TIP: Where you find fruits in the grocery store is where they should be at your house. For example, apples are never refrigerated at the store, so you can leave them out at home.

THE TABLE THAT CONNECTS

We were not meant to do life alone. God wants each of us to have thriving, edifying, life-giving relationships—a full arsenal of friends in your community. In a society that promotes individualism, we stay busy and disconnected. We are constantly seeking validation from social media, which causes us to be overwhelmed and detached.

We live in a world where communication has never been easier, yet it seems like the more ways we can communicate with each other, the less connected we have become.

Community is how God designed us to grow. Look at one of the first things Jesus did in His ministry. He created His community with twelve disciples. Jesus invited men to walk alongside Him. He built a tribe. He invested in them daily. Then, in Acts 2, it describes the early church community. "And they devoted themselves to the apostles' teaching and the fellowship, to the breaking of bread and the prayers" (Acts 2:42 ESV). The role of community in the Christian life is vital to walking deeper with Christ.

However, community only happens when we invite people in—when we open our homes and love them through all of life's moments. It provides us a safe place to pray with one another (Ephesians 6:18), serve one another in times of joy and suffering (John 13:2–10), and consistently love one another through doing life together (Ecclesiastes 4:12). God gives us the incredible privilege of witnessing how building God-centered community points people back to Him. And community, in its truest form, puts the gospel and the character of God on display.

John Piper said, "Christian friendships exist for this, namely, to say things that keep each other believing."

We need our communities to help us walk through everyday life, to be with us during the highs and lows, and to steer us back to God when we fall (because, let's face it, we all fall). Are you ready to build your community? Have you thought about what it might look like to invite coworkers, friends, acquaintances, or maybe even strangers over? Now, I'm not saying to be unsafe, but I am encouraging you to open your home to anyone who wants to come. Encourage your friends to bring their friends, and those friends to bring new friends. Who knows? Your community could come from two or three everyday get-togethers.

Think about it: What if God is waiting for you to step into action? Community is built in the small and simple moments of conversation and openness. When we come together authentically and share all our broken pieces, our joys and triumphs, our loves and losses, togetherness happens. Community is a by-product of our vulnerability, and it is exactly what God desired for His creation.

Being in a community provides the opportunity to love people like Jesus loved us (John 15:12). When we gather together, even in the everyday get-together, Jesus is there. Building this community takes one step. It starts with courageously asking, "Anyone want to get together?" At that moment, friendship is born and strengthened. What is keeping you from asking that question?

FOOD FOR THOUGHT:

How connected are you to a Christian community?
Who is someone in your life who needs true Godly connection?
How can you connect with people? Don't just think about how you can do it; actually do it. Commit to inviting two people over in the next few weeks.

ESPRESSO BALLS

Several years ago, I mentored a group of girls and loved having them over on Saturday mornings and Sunday afternoons. We always drank coffee together. I wanted to cook something for them that would be "fancy" without taking forever to make, but the only things I knew how to make at the time were cinnamon rolls and sausage biscuits. These rich and delicious espresso balls were perfect paired with our coffee.

Prep: 5 min. | **Cook: 0 min.** | **Ready In: 15 min.** | **Makes 24 (1 inch) balls**

INGREDIENTS

1 cup old-fashioned rolled oats

2 tablespoons ground flaxseed (also called flaxseed meal)

Pinch of salt

1 tablespoon espresso powder

1 tablespoon hot water

3 tablespoons real maple syrup (the stronger the flavor, the better)

1 teaspoon pure vanilla extract

½ cup plus 2 tablespoons peanut butter*

1 cup powdered sugar, for dusting

OPTIONAL:

2 tablespoons cocoa powder

2 tablespoons mini semi-sweet or dark chocolate chips

Pinch of cinnamon

*I like to heat my peanut butter in the microwave for 15–20 seconds before adding it to the mixture so it's smooth and doesn't make everything super sticky.

INSTRUCTIONS

1. In a large mixing bowl, whisk together oats, cocoa powder (if desired), ground flaxseed, salt, and semi-sweet or dark chocolate chips, if desired.

2. In a separate bowl mix together espresso powder, water, real maple syrup, pure vanilla extract, and cinnamon (only if you want…but you will want).

3. Add the espresso mixture and peanut butter to the oat mixture and combine to form a batter that resembles a really stiff cookie dough.

4. Roll into a ball just shy of golf ball size (about 1 tablespoon).

5. Dust with powdered sugar and serve these up to your friends.

PRO TIP:

If you want a sharp chocolate flavor, add the cocoa powder; if you prefer a sweeter and lighter espresso ball, make them without the cocoa powder.

CINNAMON PULL-APART BREAD

I love a good cinnamon roll. However, when having one guest over for coffee, making a full breakfast pastry seems a bit much. So I developed this very easy recipe that starts with crescent rolls and uses only 4 ingredients. It takes all of 10 minutes to put together, and then all you have to do is let it bake. This is a great pull-apart bread to put in your arsenal of easy recipes to make when you know you will have guests over!

Prep: 10 min. | **Cook: 45 min.** | **Ready In: 55 min.** | **Serves: 8–10**

INGREDIENTS

2 cans refrigerated crescent roll dough (I like to use the sheet dough, but crescent rolls will work fine as well)

1½ cup granulated sugar

2 tablespoons ground cinnamon

1 tablespoon ground nutmeg

½ cup butter, melted

FOR GLAZE:

3 tablespoons butter, melted

½ cup powdered sugar

1–2 tablespoon milk

Pinch of salt

INSTRUCTIONS

1. Preheat oven to 425 degrees F and grease a loaf pan.

2. Roll out both crescent roll dough sheets side by side.

3. In a bowl mix together butter, sugar, cinnamon, and nutmeg.

4. Evenly spread the cinnamon mixture over both sheets of dough.

5. Slice dough into squares that fit the loaf pan you have (between 3"x3" and 4"x4") and place in your greased loaf pan from front to back so they are "standing up."

6. Top with foil and place loaf pan in the oven. Bake for 25–30 minutes, remove foil, and finish baking for 15–20 minutes.

7. Use a knife to loosen the bread from the edges of the loaf pan and invert onto a clean board. Place cake plate on top of the inverted loaf, and carefully flip so it's right side up.

8. Add the glaze and serve hot while you share God's love.

TO MAKE THE GLAZE:

1. Mix together ingredients until smooth.

2. Place in a ziplock bag and snip a corner to drizzle the glaze over the bread.

3. Bread is best served the same day, but it can be wrapped and kept at room temperature for up to 2 days.

COFFEE CAKE KNOTS

I had a mentor in college who made coffee cake every Saturday morning. As we would sit in her home in Waco, Texas, that cake kept us there for hours as she poured godly wisdom into me. You could say that I owe my spiritual growth to coffee cake that year. When I moved to South Carolina I knew I had to replicate it somehow, and I came up with these poppable treats!

Prep: 15 min. | **Cook: 20 min.**
Ready In: 35 min. | **Serves: 10–12**

INGREDIENTS

1 lb. pizza dough
(store-bought or homemade)

3 tablespoons unsalted butter, melted

¼ cup brown sugar

¼ cup espresso powder

½ cup granulated sugar

2 tablespoons ground cinnamon

STREUSEL TOPPING:

1 cup brown sugar, packed

1 cup all-purpose flour

1 teaspoon ground cinnamon

Pinch of kosher salt

1 stick (½ cup) unsalted butter, very soft

INSTRUCTIONS

1. Preheat oven to 375 degrees F and grease a baking sheet.

2. On a lightly floured surface roll out the pizza dough. Brush 2 tablespoons of butter on the dough and sprinkle on the following ingredients: brown sugar, espresso powder, granulated sugar, ground cinnamon.

3. Fold the dough in half and cut the dough in 12 equal strips. Take each strip and tie an over-under knot.

4. Place the knots on the greased baking sheet.

TO MAKE THE STREUSEL:

1. In a small bowl combine flour, brown sugar, cinnamon, and salt. Use a fork to mash the butter into the mixture until completely combined and crumbly.

2. Take the remaining tablespoon of butter and brush the top of each knot. Sprinkle the streusel on each knot.

3. Bake for 18–20 minutes until the knots are golden brown.

4. Serve hot with coffee and enjoy pouring into someone's life.

ICED MOCHA ESPRESSO

This recipe is the perfect addition to having friends over on a Saturday morning or Sunday afternoon (both great times to build your community). In moments when you want to celebrate with coffee or have a special treat, use this as your go-to!

Prep: 5 min. | **Cook: 0 min.** | **Ready In: 10–15 min.** | **Serves: 12**

INGREDIENTS

6 cups iced coffee

¼ cup + 1 tablespoon sugar

2 cups heavy whipping cream

½ teaspoon vanilla

2 tablespoons cocoa powder

Dash of salt

½ quart vanilla ice cream

½ quart chocolate ice cream

INSTRUCTIONS

1. Combine iced coffee, sugar, heavy whipping cream, vanilla, cocoa powder, and salt until frothy. Set aside.

2. Using an ice cream scoop, scoop both ice creams into bottom of punch bowl. Pour coffee mixture over them. Gently stir to partially melt the ice cream.

3. Serve immediately with a big smile!

TABLE TALK WITH ABBY

Whether you gather with friends to watch reality TV or meet with the girls for book clubs, there are so many different reasons to connect with other people during the week. I would encourage you to get creative. I decided to include these specific moments in the book because it's important for you to begin identifying even a simple game night as a way to connect with people and build community. Add a layer of food to the agenda and you have all the ingredients for creating an evening full of intentional conversation and moments that deepen friendships.

PRO TIP:
These are meant to be easy recipes, so don't overcomplicate them!
It's not about how perfect the food is—it's about having the food.

POPCORN BOARD

I love using my charcuterie board for things other than charcuterie, and this is one of those times. Food placed on a board is a playground for people to make their own food combinations, and this popcorn snack board is a perfect game night or movie night snack option!

Based on what ingredients you put on your board, this works well as an appetizer, a snack, or even a funky dessert. It is a perfect community-building recipe.

Prep: 10–15 min. | **Cook: 0 min.** | **Ready In: 10–15 min.** | **Serves: 10–12**

INGREDIENTS

Aim for a wide assortment of ingredients when building your popcorn board. Bulk bins are great for this board, or find extra ingredients you have around the house.

POPCORN TYPES TO INCLUDE:

unsalted, salted, buttered, kettle corn, white cheddar, caramel, chocolate drizzle

ADD-INS:

nuts (salted, roasted, candied, raw, chocolate), trail mix, chocolate candies, wasabi peas, yogurt pretzels, sugared cereal

SEASONINGS IN A SHAKER (OR WITH A FUNKY SPOON):

garlic parmesan, salt, dried herbs, brown sugar, nacho cheddar, ranch, cheesy jalapeño

INSTRUCTIONS

1. Pick at least 5 different mix-ins or flavors. For example:
   - Spicy mix with wasabi peas
   - Yogurt-covered fruit
   - Sweet and salty trail mix
   - Salty nuts
   - Ranch seasoning

2. Arrange everything on your board and let everyone dig in with their own bowl or small paper bag!

   If you use a paper bag, everyone can take their creations home with them.

PRO TIP:
Different-sized bowls that are different heights will add personality and help promote visual interest in your board!

PARMESAN BACON CRACKERS

These are some of my favorite crackers. They are incredibly poppable. Perfect for game night, having friends over, or a midday snack, parmesan bacon crackers are great for when you need a treat on hand (and on hand quick). Make sure to bookmark this page—you will be making this recipe again. Trust me.

Prep: 5 min. | **Cook: 20 min.** | **Ready In: 30 min.** | **Makes: about 30 crackers**

INGREDIENTS

1 package ranch seasoning packet

1 cup grated Parmesan cheese

1 package crackers (Club Crackers™, Ritz Crackers™, you pick your favorite)

8–10 slices bacon

INSTRUCTIONS

1. Preheat oven to 350 degrees F.

2. In a mixing bowl, mix ranch seasoning and Parmesan cheese.

3. Arrange crackers on a wire rack on top of a cooking sheet about half an inch apart and sprinkle ½ of the cheese mixture on the crackers. Note: The more cheese, the better the bacon will stick.

4. Wrap each cracker with half a slice of bacon.

5. Bake for 20–25 minutes.

6. Immediately roll crackers in remaining cheese mixture.

7. Enjoy with your friends!

BLUE CHEESE BACON DIP

Blue cheese is so polarizing. I get it. Maybe you're looking at the name of this recipe and thinking, *Nope! Skip.* But I would ask you to give it a chance. What I love about this recipe is that we combine cream with sour cream and cream cheese to mellow out the bitterness of this cheese dip. If you still don't like it, squeeze half a lemon on it. Trust me on this one! This is a great cheese dip to take to tailgating parties.

Prep: 5 min. | **Cook: 20 min.** | **Ready In: 25 min.** | **Serves: 12**

INGREDIENTS

1 8-ounce package cream cheese, softened

⅓ cup half-and-half

5 ounces crumbled blue cheese

6 slices cooked thick-cut bacon

2 tablespoons fresh chives, chopped

1 teaspoon kosher salt

Assorted crackers

INSTRUCTIONS

1. Preheat oven to 375 degrees F

2. Beat cream cheese and half-and-half together until smooth.

3. Stir in bacon, blue cheese, and chives.

4. Spread dip into a skillet or baking dish and bake for 20 minutes.

5. Serve warm or cold with crackers in the middle of the table while playing a fun game!

PRO TIP:

Top with additional chives for an added touch.
Can also be served warm with fruit like apples, pears, and grapes.

BISCUIT TACOS

These biscuits are the bomb. They take tacos to an entirely new level and are literally amazing! You will have your book in one hand and your taco in the other. Building community is easy when you bring these to the table. Serve these with a small dish of sour cream and your friends will love you forever. Pro Tip: Make a double batch!

Prep: 10 min. | **Cook: 15 min.** | **Ready In: 25 min.** | **Serves: 8**

INGREDIENTS

½ pound ground beef

½ package taco seasoning mix

⅓ cup water

1 can refrigerated biscuits
(I prefer the buttery and fluffy grands)

¼ cup Ro-Tel™ (diced tomatoes and green chilies), drained with a paper towel

½ cup shredded Mexican blend cheese or 2 ounces Velveeta cheese™

INSTRUCTIONS

1. Preheat oven to 375 degrees F.

2. Cook beef and drain. Add taco seasoning and water. Simmer until thick.

3. Roll each biscuit out to make a 6-inch round.

4. Add 2 tablespoons of meat, 2 tablespoons of Ro-Tel, and 2 tablespoons of cheese into each round.

5. Fold the dough in half over the mixture and press to seal.

6. Place on greased cooking sheet and bake for 12 minutes or until golden brown.

7. Take out, serve with sour cream, and spend some time with old and new friends.

CHICKEN SALAD BOWLS

What I love about this recipe is that it combines two of my favorite foods—chicken salad and crescent rolls. This is such an easy recipe and makes chicken salad a little bit more elevated, fancy, and fun for your friends at book club! It's also an easy all-in-one sandwich-style food. Your friends will love it, and it will be easy to clean up!

Prep: 10 min. | **Cook: 12 min.** | **Ready In: 25 min.** | **Serves: 16**

INGREDIENTS

3–4 cups rotisserie chicken, cut or shredded to your liking

2 stalks celery, chopped

3 whole green onions, chopped

1 cup grapes, quartered

½ cup mayonnaise

½ cup plain yogurt

¼ cup half-and-half

1 lemon, juiced

1 tablespoon brown sugar

2 teaspoons salt

¼ cup fresh dill, minced

½ cup chopped pecans

½ cup dried cranberries

Salt and pepper to taste (Note: It will take more salt than you think.)

2 packages crescent roll sheet dough

INSTRUCTIONS

TO MAKE THE CHICKEN SALAD:

1. Chop all the fruits and veggies and combine with chicken in a bowl.

2. Combine mayonnaise, yogurt, lemon juice, half and half, brown sugar, and 2 teaspoons salt in a bowl (this is the dressing).

3. Add fresh dill to the dressing and taste to ensure it is salty enough for you. (I always end up adding more salt.)

4. When the dressing tastes just right, combine everything together.

5. Voilà!

TO MAKE THE CHICKEN SALAD BOWLS:

1. Preheat oven to 375 degrees F. Lightly spray regular-size muffin pan with cooking spray.

2. Unroll dough and cut sheet to make 8 equal squares. Line each muffin cup with 1 dough square.

3. Bake 10–12 minutes and then remove from oven. The crescent rolls will be puffy in the center, so as soon as you remove them from the oven you will need to flatten the centers. I use the bottom of a seasonings jar because it fits in my muffin pans.

4. Remove crescent roll cups from pan, let cool, and fill each with a scoop of chilled chicken salad.

5. Share these with your friends. But beware: they might want seconds!

NOTE: Timing does not include the time it takes to make chicken salad.

MEXICAN STREET CORN FRITTERS

In my group of friends, Mexican food is always a hit. To spice up your staples of cheese dip and tacos, these Mexican corn fritters are the perfect swap. Your friends will be raving over them! And if you make them thin enough, they get crunchy like a potato skin. Yum!

Prep: 5 min. | Cook: 10 min.
Ready In: 20 min. | Makes: 32 fritters

INGREDIENTS

FOR THE FRITTERS:

1 large egg

½ cup half-and-half

⅓ cup fine cornmeal

⅓ cup all-purpose flour

2 teaspoons of your favorite taco seasoning

1 teaspoon kosher salt

¼ cup green onions, finely chopped

2 cups corn kernels

1 cup queso fresco, crumbled

2 tablespoons olive oil

FOR THE SOUR CREAM:

½ cup sour cream

2 teaspoons lime juice

2 tablespoons fresh cilantro

½ teaspoon salt

INSTRUCTIONS

1. Make the sour cream sauce and chill until ready to serve.

2. In a medium bowl, whisk the egg and half-and-half until well combined.

3. Then whisk to combine the cornmeal, flour, and seasonings.

4. Add the green onion, corn, and queso fresco. Corn mixture should be the consistency of thick pancake batter.

5. Heat the olive oil over medium heat. Use a tablespoon to spoon the mixture into the pan. Cook until golden brown, about 2 minutes on each side.

6. Remove from pan and place on a paper towel.

7. Serve topped with sour cream sauce and corn topping as you gather with your friends.

HIBISCUS SPRITZER

A special drink is always a fun addition to any gathering, and this spritzer is easy, refreshing, tart, and not overly sweet. In the summer months when people get together and want a drink that says, "It's summer," this is that drink.

Prep: 5 min. | **Cook: 5 min.** | **Ready In: 10 min.** | **Serves: 8**

INGREDIENTS

FOR HIBISCUS SIMPLE SYRUP:

1 cup water

1 cup sugar

2 tablespoons dried hibiscus flowers (I took mine out of hibiscus tea bags that I found at the store)

FOR 1 SPRITZER:

2 tablespoons frozen orange juice

1 ounce hibiscus simple syrup

1 ounce freshly squeezed lime juice

2–3 ounces sparkling water (for this drink I like a blood orange sparkling water)

FOR A PITCHER (8–10 DRINKS):

1 cup hibiscus simple syrup

1 12-ounce can frozen orange juice

1 cup lime juice

3–4 cups sparkling water

Top with lime slices

INSTRUCTIONS

1. Make the hibiscus simple syrup. (Note: I've found a syrup at a local kitchen shop—you don't necessarily need to make the syrup.) Combine the water, sugar, and hibiscus and bring to a boil over high heat. Stir until sugar has melted, let cool, and then strain into a glass jar. Will keep in fridge for 2 weeks.

2. Combine everything. If you are making one drink, combine in a glass and add ice. If you are making the pitcher, combine in the pitcher and chill until ready to serve over ice.

3. It is always nice to serve with fresh slices of fruit on the top.

BRUSCHETTA BAR

Charcuterie is so popular and festive. But it can often be more expensive and not as filling as other appetizers. That is why I am sharing this Italian bruschetta bar. Complete with dips, breads, and meats, this twist on a charcuterie board lets everyone make their own "open-faced sandwich" or bruschetta.

Interesting fact: Bruschetta is actually in the Italian antipasto family and is traditionally a piece of grilled bread rubbed with garlic and topped with olive oil and salt. More modern bruschetta variations include topping the grilled bread with tomato, veggies, beans, olives, cured meat, and cheese.

Prep: 5 min. | Cook: 5 min. | Ready In: 10 min. | Serves: 10–12

INGREDIENTS

These are just suggestions for a great bruschetta board. Everything below has a Mediterranean/Italian feel.

1 large loaf French bread sliced into ½-inch pieces

Olive oil for drizzling (I like olive oil in a spray bottle for this)

2 tablespoons garlic salt

Sun-dried tomatoes

Sautéed mushrooms

Basil pesto

Burrata

Marinated olives

Cured meats like pepperoni and prosciutto

Fresh greens like arugula

Red pesto hummus

INSTRUCTIONS

1. Set your oven to broil—set it to high if you have that option.

2. Drizzle olive oil on both sides of the bread and salt each side. Put in the oven on a cookie sheet for a minute or two and then flip the bread to the other side. Let it broil for just another minute—be careful not to burn.

3. Remove and set to the side.

4. Place all the toppings on a large platter and serve with the grilled bread. I like to put my add-ons in small bowls to keep flavors from merging on the board.

5. I hope you enjoy this with new friends! As they build their bruschetta, you are building community.

GOAT CHEESE BALLS WITH HONEY AND ROSEMARY

Raise your hand if you grew up enjoying fried mozzarella sticks...and still do sometimes. This recipe is the "fancy-adult" equivalent of the fried mozz stick! Just imagine a basket full of fried goat cheese with a drizzle of honey and rosemary on it. I'd say yes to that as my snack of choice all day. And your friends will agree.

Prep: 20 min. | **Cook: 10 min.**
Ready In: 30 min. | **Serves: 10–12**

INGREDIENTS

⅓ cup all-purpose flour

1 large egg, beaten

2 tablespoons water

1½ cups panko bread crumbs

1 teaspoon salt

10 ounces goat cheese

Oil for frying

Rosemary sprigs for serving

Enough honey for drizzling

INSTRUCTIONS

1. Add flour to a bowl.

2. Add egg and 2 tablespoons water to a separate bowl. Whisk together.

3. Add bread crumbs and salt to a third medium-sized bowl.

4. Roll the log of goat cheese into 20–24 balls (about 1 tablespoon each).

5. Roll each ball in the flour, then in the egg mixture, and finally through the bread crumbs. Place each ball on the sheet pan, then freeze for 20 minutes.

6. Heat 1–2 inches of oil in a large skillet over medium-high heat. Fry the goat cheese balls for 1–2 minutes or until golden brown on all sides.

7. Remove and place on a paper towel.

8. Arrange on a serving plate with sprigs of rosemary, and drizzle honey over each ball.

9. Best if served warm with your tribe around you.

MEDITERRANEAN GALETTE

I'm always down for a good pizza, especially if I know the girls are coming over and we are needing cheese and carbs to accompany late-night conversations. The first galette I ever made was a dessert galette. It was a sweet berry galette and a super tasty alternative to pie. Then, I worked on a savory version by adding my favorite Mediterranean ingredients to the base, and it was amazing. Invite your girlfriends over this weekend and try this pizza-pie hybrid. You will not regret it, and this will be your new go-to comfort pie.

Prep: 5 min. | Cook: 0 min.
Ready In: 10-15 min. | Serves: 12

INGREDIENTS

Pie crust, refrigerated

2 tablespoons olive oil, add extra for drizzling

1 tablespoon garlic paste

1 jar marinated artichoke hearts

6 marinated olives, halved

6–8 slices prosciutto

1 tablespoon lemon juice

Salt and pepper to taste

2 teaspoons Italian seasoning

¼ cup sun-dried tomatoes

6 ounces spinach

2-3 leaves fresh basil, sliced

4 ounces goat cheese, crumbled

1 egg for egg wash (whisk 1 egg & 1 tablespoon water together)

INSTRUCTIONS

1. Preheat the oven to 425 degrees F.

2. Unroll the pie dough onto a baking sheet or pizza stone.

3. Heat 2 tablespoons of olive oil in a pan and sauté the garlic. Cook for 1 minute on low heat until fragrant. Garlic has a low burning point—be careful not to burn it.

4. Remove from heat and add artichoke hearts, olives, prosciutto, lemon juice, salt and pepper, Italian seasoning, and sun-dried tomatoes. Toss in the spinach and basil.

5. Place the mixture in the middle of the pie dough, leaving roughly 2 inches around the edges. Top with goat cheese crumbles.

6. Grab the dough at the edges and fold it over to the center. Lightly brush the edges with the egg wash.

7. Bake for 20 minutes.

8. Remove, let cool, and drizzle with olive oil, then serve around the table echoing with laughter.

FROZEN APPETIZER BOARD

If you haven't figured it out already, I love wooden cutting boards. I use them for charcuterie, bread, and even a throw-and-go appetizer board. Every time I make this board for friends, it is a hit. Best part—it is really easy and comes together super fast. It's also something you can keep on hand, just in case you don't have time to go to the store before friends come over. You know, that occasional last-minute girlfriend get-together? Grab your favorite cutting board and favorite frozen apps out of the freezer and this comes together in minutes.

Prep: 5 min. | Cook: 10–20 min. | Ready In: 30 min. | Serves: 10–12

INGREDIENTS

INCLUDE SOME DIPS:

Ketchup

Sour cream

Pimento cheese

FROZEN APPETIZERS:

Potato skins

Taquitos

Savory puff pastry bites

Meatballs

Buffalo chicken tenders

ADD SOME FRESHNESS TO THE BOARD:

Carrots

Celery

Sweet Peppers

Cucumbers

INSTRUCTIONS

1. Place all the prepared appetizers, dips, and fresh veggies on a large platter or board and serve.

2. Don't forget to invite all the friends! This is a great recipe for all the friends, not just the girls!

RO TIP:

When you are serving anything on a board, try to vary the sizes, shapes, and colors of your appetizers. This can be challenging because a lot of frozen appetizers are brown. But that is why I'm here—to help inspire you!

FRENCH PUNCH

Having everyone over to watch a movie and chill on the weekend is one of my favorite ways to hang out. Rarely do we finish the movie because we just have so much fun talking. There were times in life when I would pray for that kind of community. I'm so thankful for the friendships I have, and when I have the chance to have friends over, I love to have this pitcher of French punch ready. It's just perfect for a night with the girls.

Prep: 10 min. | Cook: 0 min. | Ready In: 10 min. | Serves: 8–10

INGREDIENTS

3 cups strawberries, sliced

¾ cup simple syrup

1 12-ounce can frozen lemonade

2 12-ounce cans ginger ale or strawberry soda (I recommend Fanta)

Sliced strawberries and lemon peels for a nice addition to the pitcher

INSTRUCTIONS

1. Blend strawberries and simple syrup into a puree. Strain into a serving pitcher.

2. Add the frozen lemonade and ginger ale. Stir in the sliced strawberries and lemon peels.

3. Add ice to glasses and serve!

NOTE: To make simple syrup use equal parts water and sugar. Combine the water and sugar and bring to a boil over high heat. Stir until sugar has melted, let cool, and then strain into a glass jar. Will keep in fridge for 2 weeks.

GREEK FRENCH FRY BASKET

Sometimes all you need is to spice up some store-bought french fries. Now, yes, I could walk you through the slicing process and how to bake potatoes to get them to the perfect crunch. But how much easier is it to walk into the frozen aisle of your nearest grocery store, pick up some frozen fries, bring them home, and top them with some fun ingredients? That is what I love most about this recipe. It takes something super basic, adds a fun twist, and makes serving food to your friends easy and effortless!

Prep: 5 min. | **Cook: 30 min.**
Ready In: 40 min. | **Serves: 10–12**

INGREDIENTS

1 14-ounce bag shoestring fries

¼ cup olive oil

1 teaspoon dried oregano

1 teaspoon dried basil

1 teaspoon fresh basil, minced

Salt and pepper to taste

3 teaspoons garlic paste

6 ounces feta cheese, crumbled

Fresh basil, for garnish

Optional: Tzatziki sauce for serving

INSTRUCTIONS

1. Preheat oven to 450 degrees F.
2. Place fries in a large bowl and coat with oil.
3. Mix in the seasonings, salt and pepper, and garlic.
4. Spread the fries on a baking sheet in an even layer. You might need 2 cooking sheets.
5. Bake for 15–20 minutes, then flip fries and bake until done. I like mine a bit crispier, so mine tend to stay in a bit longer.
6. Remove from oven and toss with fresh basil and feta cheese.
7. Serve with Tzatziki sauce.

NOTE: I have transitioned to using my air fryer for these fries. It takes between 8 and 10 minutes, and they are super tasty and are done in a fraction of the time!

TO USE AIR FRYER:

1. Preheat air fryer to 400 degrees F.
2. Put fries in basket and shake every 2-3 minutes.
3. Let them cook for 8–10 minutes.

THE TABLE THAT TEACHES

God created us to share our lives with others. He basically starts the Bible by saying, "It is not good for the man to be alone" (Genesis 2:18 NIV). This specific Scripture is talking about creating Eve for Adam, but it also shows God's desire for us to live in community with other people. He gave each of us a longing for connection. This is why even the most introverted individual wants to share their life with a few close friends. We all know that being alone in this world can lead to feelings of abandonment and heartache. That is why, in our busy lives, we must arm ourselves with community. And how do we create community? Well, sometimes it's as simple as opening your front door and inviting someone to your table.

Community is inclusive in a world that preaches exclusivity. I would like to propose a definition of building community. I believe building your community, at its core, is facilitating the inclusion of people.

The story of Jesus feeding the five thousand (Matthew 14:13–21) gives us a sense of how Jesus used food to draw people in.

Jesus wasn't worried about the number of people or the presentation of food, or even what He was feeding them. He was concerned about the hearts and souls of each person there and the relationship He desired to have with them. The mere thought of feeding five thousand people can distract us from His purpose that day. We can get so caught up in the food, presentation, and Insta-worthy tablescape that we forget that sometimes we just need to connect with people. So, find your people and feed them, not just with food but with love and grace—just like Jesus did.

Use the table—not just as a place where bread is broken but where deep conversations happen. It's the place where God weaves together everyday moments with grace, laughter, joy, friendship, redemption, and, most importantly, love.

It's easy to remember that Jesus fed five thousand people with only five loaves of bread and two fish. But, do you know what happened at the end of the story? What about the leftovers? Mark 6:43 tells us the leftovers were for the people serving the food. I think Jesus was teaching the servers (the disciples) that He would provide for them. When you trust in God, He will provide more than you can imagine (Ephesians 3:20 NIV). There is no way you can out-give or out-serve Jesus. When you understand that, your mindset begins to shift from inward selfishness to outward service. When you commit to serving others and opening your home, you commit to allowing God to provide. It challenges us to continually strive to embody and live out the gospel. When you serve others, Jesus will take care of the rest. He will do so and still have some left over.

Hosting people in your home does not require perfection; in fact, hosting someone when our home is imperfect requires us to be vulnerable, open, and authentic. This "imperfect hospitality" is sometimes received better than an attempt at being picture perfect with amazing decor and a perfect food spread. Dishes don't need to match, decor doesn't have to be perfectly placed, and your food doesn't even need to be elaborate. When Jesus sat to have lunch with five thousand on that hill that day, He didn't bring any food. It could seem like Jesus wasn't prepared; however, because His heart was prepared, He was able to open His arms and welcome people in. He calls us to do the same, to open our homes and sit at the table. Be who God created you to be and watch Him create perfect moments from your imperfect table.

100 DAYS OF

FOOD FOR THOUGHT:

What step of faith is God asking you to take to serve others? Does that intimidate you? Why?
If you knew that community would flourish in your home if you opened your doors and prepared food, how would you live differently? What is holding you back?
Who is someone in your life you can serve at your table this week or maybe this month?

TABLE TALK WITH ABBY

Life is crazy. Not just sometimes but all the time. That's why we all need a place to go where we feel comfortable to be ourselves, to share our innermost thoughts, and to be heard and understood and safe. For me, this is my community group at church. When I surround myself with my small group of believers, I feel reenergized. This group of women not only hear my worries, thoughts, and prayers, but they point me back to God, who is always there with open arms. Jeremiah 24:7 NLT says "I will give them hearts that recognize Me as the Lord. They will be my people, and I will be their God, for they will return to Me wholeheartedly." God desires us to be drawn into His presence, into a relationship with Him. When we deepen our relationship with Him, He gives us a heart to serve and love others. Do you have people to love and encourage? If not, maybe it's time to open your home and invite a few people to study the Bible with you. Maybe even start a potluck dinner club! After all, building community by growing spiritually together is how you create a bond that will last forever.

The recipes in this section are perfect for hosting small groups of people. So, let's start cooking and connecting!

BLUEBERRY BALSAMIC GOAT CHEESE SPREAD

It took a while, but I finally found a really good cheese dip that feels more tea party than tailgate. It's a simple recipe with a mouth-watering blend of sweet and savory.

Prep: 5 min. | **Cook: 10 min.** | **Ready In: 15 min.** | **Serves: 10–12**

INGREDIENTS

1 cup blueberries, fresh or frozen

1 sprig fresh rosemary

2 teaspoons honey

1 teaspoon salt

2 teaspoons balsamic vinegar

1 10-ounce goat cheese log

2 ounces cream cheese, slightly melted

Serve with crostini, crackers, fresh French bread

INSTRUCTIONS

1. In a saucepan over medium heat. Combine the blueberries, rosemary sprig, honey, salt, and balsamic vinegar. Cook for 10 minutes, stirring occasionally. You want the blueberries to pop and create a thick sauce. If it looks thin, it will thicken more when you remove from the heat.

2. Remove from heat, take out the rosemary sprig and toss, and allow to cool.

3. In a medium bowl mix the goat cheese and cream cheese together.

4. Spread the goat cheese mixture in a plate or bowl and top with the blueberry mixture.

5. Serve warm and enjoy with your friends while soaking up God's Word.

S'MORES POPCORN

One thing I have learned about getting together with women is that we talk more when we have a bowl of munchies in front of us. My college roommates and I would always bring our favorite add-ins for trail mix when we wanted to spend intentional time with each other. This popcorn recipe reminds me of those special times. It reminds me that intentional conversation can happen, but it happens easier with munchies. To get that sweet and sticky crunch of a s'more, you don't even have to have a fire! Be intentional—this recipe will help you.

Prep: 15 min. | **Cook: 0 min.**
Ready In: 15 min. | **Serves: 10–12**

INGREDIENTS

6 cups popped popcorn

2 cups mini marshmallows

2 Hershey's chocolate bars, diced

3 cups broken graham crackers

1 cup semisweet chocolate chips

INSTRUCTIONS

1. Combine popcorn, marshmallows, diced chocolate, and broken graham crackers in a bowl and mix together.

2. Spread evenly on parchment paper.

3. Melt semisweet chocolate in a microwave-safe bowl for 30 seconds. Remove from microwave and give it a stir. Continue this process 30 seconds at a time until all chocolate is melted to avoid burning.

4. Drizzle chocolate over the mixture and allow to harden.

5. Serve and enjoy a lot more conversation with this bowl of munchies!

5-INGREDIENT BEER BREAD

Bread can be intimidating because of the ingredients, the process, the perfection of it all. This recipe is one of my favorites because of its simplicity. It doesn't have to be perfect; in fact, the way it rises exudes imperfection. That's kind of how we are with Christ. Even when we aren't perfect, God is still good—just like this bread.

Prep: 10 min. | **Cook: 1 hour** | **Ready In: 1 hour and 10 min.** | **Serves: 8–10**

INGREDIENTS

3 cups self-rising flour

3 tablespoons sugar

1½ tablespoons baking powder

12 ounces beer (1 bottle)

6 tablespoons salted butter

INSTRUCTIONS

1. Preheat oven to 375 degrees F.

2. Mix flour, sugar, baking powder, and beer together in a mixer until it gets sticky and pulls away from the bowl.

3. Place dough in a greased loaf pan.

4. Drizzle melted butter on top—don't mix or incorporate.

5. Bake for 1 hour and allow to cool on wire rack before serving.

OLIVE TAPENADE HUMMUS

I love loaded hummus appetizers. There is something so satisfying about this Middle Eastern cuisine with toppings. And I haven't met anyone who doesn't like this dip. You don't necessarily need to make the olive tapenade, but it is so much more delicious if you do, and it only takes about 10 additional minutes to put it together.

Prep: 20 min. | **Cook: 0 min.** | **Ready In: 20 min.** | **Serves: 8–10**

INGREDIENTS

OLIVE TAPENADE INGREDIENTS:

2½ cups olives—I choose a mix of black kalamata, green, and marinated, all pitted and drained

2 tablespoons capers, drained

3 tablespoons sun-dried tomatoes, drained and patted dry

2 tablespoons minced garlic

1 teaspoon dried oregano

4 tablespoons fresh parsley

1 tablespoon fresh basil

1 teaspoon black pepper

2 tablespoons lemon juice

¼ cup extra virgin olive oil

HUMMUS INGREDIENTS:

12–16 ounces garlic hummus

¾ cup olive tapenade

1 tablespoon Za'atar, optional topping

INSTRUCTIONS

1. Add olives, capers, tomatoes, seasonings, lemon juice, and olive oil to food processor.

2. Pulse until you get a fine and chunky texture. I prefer my tapenade to be a bit more fine than chunky, which produces more oil.

3. Serve immediately with a big smile!

TO PREPARE THE HUMMUS:

• Spread 10 ounces of garlic hummus on a plate.

• Top with olive tapenade.

• I like to sprinkle the top of the finished dish with a little Za'atar and pine nuts.

NOTES:

• Fresh tapenade will last in the fridge for about 2 weeks. If left longer, the olives will become rancid and lose their flavor.

• Za'atar is a Middle Eastern blend of seasonings that includes dried herbs like oregano, marjoram, and thyme as well as cumin and coriander blended with sumac and sesame seeds. I fell in love with it in Israel and am always looking for a way to incorporate it into my recipes!

CHEESEBURGER DIP

I know what you're thinking: *Why not just make burgers?* But trust me, with this recipe, it's easy cleanup and the flavor in every bite will make you second-guess every other snack you've ever served. Once a week I hang out with a group of eighth-grade girls, and I love it. To be honest, I wish I could have benefited from a mentorship relationship when I was in middle school. My outlook on life while I was growing up could have been drastically different. Growing in community, friendships, and intentional conversation shapes our lives—starting at a young age. Don't overlook opportunities to love on kids with food!

Prep: 15 min. | **Cook: 15 min.** | **Ready In: 30 min.** | **Serves: 10–12**

INGREDIENTS

½ pound ground beef

½ yellow onion, chopped (consider buying pre-chopped onions)

8 ounces cream cheese, softened

¼ cup sliced dill pickles

1 Roma tomato, seeded and diced

2 tablespoons Worcestershire sauce

¾ cup sour cream

1 teaspoon garlic powder

1 teaspoon salt

½ teaspoon black pepper

1 cup shredded cheddar cheese

INSTRUCTIONS

1. Cook meat with onions in a greased skillet (about 5 minutes).

2. Add everything else but the cheese and stir until saucy.

3. Add cheddar cheese and stir.

4. I serve mine with sliced hamburger buns that I toast in the oven.

5. Serve straight out of the skillet with slider bread— less mess that way!

NOTES:

- Will last in fridge for up to 4 days.
- You can also make this recipe in your slow cooker.

BROWNIE COOKIES

When I am thinking about recipes for parties, I like to have my arsenal of sweet treats. Most of the time I go with a tried-and-true chocolate chip cookie. What I have learned is that the best conversation comes with chocolate, and you can't get enough of the chocolate in these brownie cookies!

Prep: 20 min. | **Cook: 0 min.** | **Ready In: 20 min.** | **Serves: 8–10**

INGREDIENTS

1 box double chocolate chunk brownie mix

2 eggs

¼ cup vegetable oil

¼ cup flour

¼ cup water

1 cup milk chocolate chips

INSTRUCTIONS

1. Preheat oven to 325 degrees F.

2. Line a cookie sheet with parchment paper.

3. Mix all ingredients except the chocolate chips.

4. Drop 1 tablespoon-sized balls of mix onto cookie sheet.

5. Place as many chocolate chips on the top of each cookie as desired. Make sure to press them into the cookie. It's okay if they are close together—the cookie dough will spread out as it bakes.

6. Bake for 10 minutes or until cooked. I watch mine closely because brownies are best when they are a bit gooey on the inside.

7. Remove and let cool for 5–10 minutes, and then let everyone gobble them up!

KITCHEN SINK TRAIL MIX

This is one of my favorite things to do with my students when they come over for Bible study or just to gather and chat. I ask each student to bring 1 cup of their favorite small snack. When they come over they get to add their ingredient to the trail mix. Stir it up and share it out. It's a perfect example of how God created community. Romans 12:5 reminds us that even though there are many of us, we are "one body in Christ" (ESV). There are lots of ingredients in this trail mix; each is important, and together they make one tasty treat. That's how we need to view and treat people—we are all different, but each person is so important.

Prep: 5 min. | Cook: 0 min. | Ready In: 5 min. | Serves: 12–16

INGREDIENTS

4 cups popped popcorn

SAMPLE INGREDIENTS INCLUDE:

1 cup mini pretzels

1 cup Goldfish™ crackers

1 cup animal crackers

1 cup cereal

1 cup dried cranberries

1 cup chocolate candies (even those miniature peanut butter cups are great)

1 cup mini sandwich cookies

1 cup mini marshmallows

INSTRUCTIONS

1. Start with a large batch of popcorn (can be store-bought—I give you permission!).

2. Add all the ingredients and stir.

3. Everyone can make their own to-go sack and fill it up! That way you aren't stuck with a ton of leftovers and everyone takes their sack with them (easy cleanup for you!).

FRENCH TOAST CASSEROLE

These are perfect for a women's conference or morning prayer gatherings on Saturday morning! Sure, you could run to the donut shop in town and grab a dozen, or (and bear with me for a minute) you could be a hero and make a mouth-watering casserole. Let's be honest, when women get together to talk, there is nothing we love more than a casserole. So try it out! It's an easy recipe that you make the night before and takes 30–45 minutes in the oven.

Prep: 20 min. | **Cook: 0 min.** | **Ready In: 20 min.** | **Serves: 8–10**

INGREDIENTS

2 loaves French bread, cut into cubes

8 large eggs

2 cups 2% milk

2 teaspoons vanilla extract

2 teaspoons cinnamon

1 teaspoon salt

¾ cup brown sugar

1 cup strawberries, sliced

½ cup blueberries

Powdered sugar, for garnish

Maple syrup, for serving

INSTRUCTIONS

1. Preheat oven to 375 degrees F.
1. Grab your 9x13 casserole dish and grease it up.
2. Cut the bread into cubes until the casserole dish is about ¾ of the way full.
3. In a bowl, mix well eggs, milk, vanilla, cinnamon, salt, and brown sugar.
4. Pour the mixture over the casserole.
5. Top casserole with sliced strawberries and fresh blueberries.
6. Refrigerate overnight.
7. Bake for about 45 minutes.
8. Top with powdered sugar and serve with maple syrup!
9. Yum!

LEMON FETA DIP

My friends know that when they come over to my house we will always have cheese. It is kind of my thing. But whether it is a block of white cheddar, a log of goat cheese, or this amazing lemon feta dip, it's not about having a perfect spread. We need to start putting to the side the expectation of perfection and begin living life with each other. This lemon feta dip helps you do just that.

Prep: 5 min. | **Cook: 5 min.**
Ready In: 10 min. | **Serves: 8–10**

INGREDIENTS

3 tablespoons olive oil

2 tablespoons garlic paste

8 ounces cream cheese, softened

8 ounces feta cheese

¼ teaspoon chili powder

½ lemon juice and zest

1 tablespoon minced chives, for garnish

INSTRUCTIONS

1. Heat 1 tablespoon of olive oil with the garlic paste until fragrant. Remember, garlic has a super low burning point, so heat on medium-low and watch carefully. It won't take long.

2. In a food processor, pulse together cream cheese, feta cheese, and chili power.

3. Add the remaining 2 tablespoons of olive oil, lemon juice and zest, and the garlic oil to mixture and pulse until smooth.

4. Spread onto a plate or bowl and garnish with minced chives and a dash of olive oil, if desired.

5. Serve with crackers or veggies, and do life with someone!

CHICKEN BACON RANCH PULL-APART SLIDERS

Everyone loves a good slider. In fact, when people get together, I can almost guarantee someone has made those ham and cheese and poppy seed sliders. So be different! If you like those sandwiches, you will die for these.

Prep: 10 min. | **Cook: 20 min.** | **Ready In: 30 min.** | **Makes: 12 Sandwiches**

INGREDIENTS

1 15-ounce package sweet Hawaiian rolls

½ cup butter

1 teaspoon garlic salt

1 tablespoon chopped fresh chives

½ teaspoon onion powder

⅓ cup ranch salad dressing

12 slices Colby-Jack cheese

1 pound chicken, deli or pulled (I prefer pulled rotisserie chicken)

12 slices bacon, cooked and crumbled

2 tablespoons Parmesan cheese

INSTRUCTIONS

1. Preheat oven to 350 degrees F.

2. Cut the Hawaiian rolls in half so you have a top and bottom. Place the bottom on a baking sheet or in a casserole dish. Set the tops aside.

3. Heat the butter until melted. Add the garlic salt, chives, and onion powder.

4. Drizzle the ranch dressing on the bottom of the rolls.

5. Layer half the cheese on the bottom, then add chicken and bacon and then the rest of the cheese.

6. Place the top on each sandwich, brush with the remaining butter, and sprinkle Parmesan cheese.

7. Bake for 20 minutes and serve warm with a side of ranch dressing

NOTE: Hawaiian bread is a sweeter bread that is made with milk, sugar, eggs, yeast, flour, and lemon. I highly recommend sticking with the Hawaiian roll for this recipe. However, it will work with regular bread.

73

THE TABLE THAT SERVES

There is one thing that we naturally gravitate towards during life's moments, be it a birthday, a wedding, a celebration: we bring food. We can learn a lot from the last night Jesus was with His disciples (Matthew 26:17–30) before He was taken to be crucified. Jesus knew what was going to happen in the following days—but He was also human. He wanted to spend that last night not on a boat fishing, not doing ministry on the mountain side or sitting alone; He wanted to spend that last night breaking bread around a table with the people He loved. You see, Jesus knew that relationships are formed at the table and God desires that connection.

We see this theme throughout Scripture, God wanting connection with His people and for His people to desire that connection back with Him. It's literally how God wired us to be and it's what makes Christianity so unique. We have a God that designed us to crave connection with Him and with others. And it's through connection with others we get a glimpse of who He is.

Luke 23:55 says, "As His body was taken away, the women from Galilee followed and saw the tomb where His body was placed" (NLT).

Jesus had just been crucified and buried, which took place in Jerusalem. These women were from Galilee. The phrase "the women from Galilee" is easy to glance over, but Galilee is seventy miles from Jerusalem. These women were serious about being there and being with Jesus. But the important part is that they were brought together by Jesus. We learn this in Luke 8. These women were brought together through miracles Jesus had performed. Jesus is ready to perform a miracle at your table, and deepen intentional relationships with people in your life. The women from Galilee had deep, God-centered relationships with each other.

Following Jesus's crucifixion these women prepared spices for Jesus's body, rested together on the Sabbath, and then went back to the tomb on Sunday (Luke 24:1–2).

They stayed together that weekend because they had been together. When life happens, the good or the bad, we stick together. People in true community live their lives together, day-in and day-out. It's not about the big events, but the small everyday moments that strengthen relationships.

When there is a crisis and your community is grounded in Christ, you rally. You don't have to go at it alone. Have you ever seen a group of women rally when there is a crisis? The text messages start flying, calendars open, and colorful gel pens start creating a meal train. Why? Because food and the table unite us. God-honoring, deep friendships are rooted in intentional service no matter the moment.

In the same vein, when we have moments in life to celebrate, women show up. We are there with cakes and pies and all sorts of goodies! We have an interconnectedness that draws us in to build each other up.

There is nothing better than having that tribe of women there when you need them. My grandfather passed away a decade or so ago, and I find myself at times identifying with my grandmother. When I've had a hard day at work or a bout with loneliness, I'll call her and say all I need today—right now—is a hug. She understands that because for fifty years she had a hug when she needed it, and she knows the importance of human connection. She will gently nudge me toward community with an encouraging "call your friends"—and my community won't just show up with a hug; they will show up with food too. As Christians,

God designed us to need each other. Knowing there are moments when we need a friend should make us hyper-aware to the fact that others will need us. And in those moments they might not be bold enough to ask for it. Be deliberate in noticing others and engaging with those around you in genuine ways. God uses us in our most vulnerable moments to show up, work through us, and make His glory known.

Jesus used the table throughout His ministry. But the significance of the table is not just about the food. It's about the literal breaking of bread, building relationships, tearing down walls and judgments, and serving each other during all of life's moments.

FOOD FOR THOUGHT:

How are you currently serving your community? Do you celebrate your friends' everyday moments in life?

Is there anything holding you back from serving people in all of life's moments?

What is one thing you've learned about God or His Word recently that can help you serve your community better?

TABLE TALK WITH ABBY

Out of all of the reasons to cook food, I must say my favorite reason is to serve my community—whether they are celebrating or mourning. No matter what is going on in life, we serve a "go and do" God. In a culture that is head down and eyes glued to a device in our hands, we can miss out on what happens when we make it a priority to serve others. I hope these recipes become your staples to prepare for others and these pages become stained with love. Pick some of your favorites, fold the pages over, and really dig into what God is calling you to do and who God is calling you to serve.

DESSERT KABOB

I absolutely love sip & sees, which are parties usually planned by new parents. It's a time for friends and family to stop by, enjoy light refreshments, and meet the new baby. Gathering together with friends to celebrate a sweet moment like a birth is amazing. One thing I love about these dessert kabobs is they use ingredients that are premade and come together super quick. They also don't require a plate, can be eaten while you are standing around talking, and are not sticky like a lot of other desserts. Win-win in my book!

Prep: 10 min. | Cook: 0 min. | Ready In: 15 min. | Makes: 10–12 kabobs

INGREDIENTS

10–12 wooden skewers

1 box mini square Rice Krispies Treats™, unwrapped

12 brownie bites (I highly recommend grabbing these from your local grocery store's bakery)

12 ounces strawberries, tops removed and sliced in half

12 roasting marshmallows

1 15-ounce cup edible cookie dough, rolled into small 1 tablespoon-sized balls

7 ounces melting chocolate (go easy on yourself and grab the microwavable dipping chocolate in a cup)

INSTRUCTIONS

1. Get the skewers ready by rinsing with hot water. Pat dry.

2. Lay out the Rice Krispies Treats™ on parchment paper and drizzle the melting chocolate on them as desired. Let cool.

3. Begin skewering the brownies, Rice Krispies Treats™, marshmallows, cookie dough, and strawberries.

4. Plate and serve. See, it is just that simple!.

NOTE: Have fun with this. Make a pattern, double up your favorite treat, or maybe drizzle more chocolate and pink or blue sprinkles to celebrate the baby.

BISCUIT BAR WITH STRAWBERRY AND MINT CHUTNEY

Kids are such a gift from God, and so is friendship. What better way to encourage the new moms in your tribe than with this biscuit bar! It's easy to transport and a great addition to any gathering where you will be happily gushing over sweet babies!

Prep: 5 min. | Cook: 45 min.
Ready In: 50 min. | Serves: 12–16

INGREDIENTS

12 southern biscuits, cooked

2 teaspoons ground ginger

1½ cups strawberries, chopped

1 cup sugar (or more, depending on taste)

1½ teaspoons salt

¼ cup water

12 leaves fresh mint, finely chopped

INSTRUCTIONS

1. Place all the ingredients (except the biscuits) in a pot over medium heat. Avoid boiling by stirring occasionally. Let strawberries cook down for 25–30 minutes. Consistency should be thick.

2. Serve on a warm, buttery biscuit.

NOTE: The amount of sugar depends on the sweetness of your strawberries. For example, at the start of the season when they are ripe, you won't need any extra sugar.

PRO TIP:

It's not about having the perfect homemade meal, it's about having food and building relationships. You have my permission to use your favorite store-bought southern biscuits and save time so you can spend that extra time with the people that matter in your life.

BLUEBERRY MINT ROYALE

Christ calls us to show up for our friends no matter what the occasion. I feel like the birth of a baby is a pretty big occasion, so show up in a big way! This blueberry mint royale will get you well on your way to celebration mode! God can use even the simplest gestures in the most profound ways. Throw a party, have friends over, and show up for people. Super basic and well worth it!

Prep: 15 min. | Cook: 10 min.
Ready In: 25 min. | Serves: 8–10

INGREDIENTS

FOR MINT SIMPLE SYRUP:

1 cup water

1 cup sugar

6 sprigs of mint

FOR 1 DRINK:

½ lime cut into wedges, for garnish

4 mint leaves

⅓ cup fresh blueberries

2 tablespoons mint simple syrup

Club soda or sparkling water to top off the glass

FOR A PITCHER (10 DRINKS):

1 cup mint simple syrup

4 limes cut into wedges

2½ cups fresh blueberries

3–4 cups club soda or sparkling water (this also works well with a blueberry pomegranate sparkling water)

Top with lime slices

INSTRUCTIONS

1. Make the mint simple syrup. (You don't necessarily have to make this. If you find a syrup you like at your grocery store, use it!) To make simple syrup: Combine the water, sugar, and mint and bring to a boil over high heat. Stir until sugar has melted, let cool, and then strain into a glass jar. Will keep in fridge for 2 weeks.

2. Combine lime wedges, mint leaves, and blueberries and muddle together (muddle means to press or smash ingredients to bring out the flavors). If making a single drink, you can muddle in the bottom of your glass. If making a pitcher, use a medium-sized bowl or food processor.

3. Add the club soda or sparkling water

4. Top with lime wedges, blueberries, and extra mint and serve over ice.

PESTO AND CHICKEN SAVORY PIE

I am a big fan of handheld food, especially when I am going to someone's house for a get-together. That is why I decided to include this savory pie in the book. It can stand alone or be coupled with chips and dip or even a salad. It is easy to make and basic enough that everyone will love it! Oh, and this recipe can be doubled or tripled. Yum!

Prep: 15 min. | Cook: 25 min. | Ready In: 40 min. | Serves: 6

INGREDIENTS

1 box (2 sheets) frozen puff pastry, thawed in the fridge

Egg wash (1 large egg beaten with 2 tablespoons water)

FILLING:

4 tablespoons pesto

½ cup cherry tomatoes, chopped

1 cup shredded chicken (a rotisserie chicken is perfect for this)

1 cup shredded mozzarella cheese

1 teaspoon salt

1 teaspoon pepper

1 cup spinach

TOPPING:

Salt and pepper to taste

2 tablespoons fresh thyme, finely chopped

INSTRUCTIONS

1. Preheat oven to 400 degrees F and grease a cookie sheet.

2. Cut puff pastry into 6 equal rectangles and prick the centers of the puff pastry rectangles with a fork.

3. Combine filling ingredients in a bowl and spoon onto the center of 3 of the puff pastry rectangles.

4. Top each bottom rectangle with one of the top puff pastry rectangles, lining them up as best as you can.

5. Crimp the edges together with a fork. Brush egg wash over each pie, and sprinkle salt, pepper, and thyme over the top of each one.

6. Bake the pies for 20–22 minutes until they have risen and are a deep golden.

7. Serve warm and enjoy all the cuddles with the new baby!

GRAPEFRUIT AND THYME MOCKTAIL

Ahh, doesn't this drink just scream "I'm with my girls"? This is the perfect drink for a bridal brunch. Everyone you invite will be sure to enjoy this tart and sweet refreshing drink! Don't have a bride to make this for? Don't worry—invite your girlfriends over for life chats. Use this drink to be intentional and invest in someone!

Prep: 5 min. | **Cook: 0 min.** | **Ready In: 5 min.** | **Serves: 4–6**

INGREDIENTS

2 cups fresh pink grapefruit juice (buy store-bought juice or juice 2 grapefruits)

½ cup simple syrup (see below for simple syrup recipe)

4 cups sparkling water

6–8 sprigs thyme

1 red grapefruit, sliced

INSTRUCTIONS

1. Combine everything together and stir.

2. In pitcher include sliced grapefruit and sprigs of thyme or serve individually in each glass.

NOTE: To make simple syrup use equal parts water and sugar. Combine the water and sugar and bring to a boil over high heat. Stir until sugar has melted, let cool, and then strain into a glass jar. Will keep in fridge for 2 weeks.

BREAKFAST BOARD

This board is a great option when you have girlfriends coming over but you aren't planning on preparing a huge meal for them. It has something for everyone—roasted breakfast potatoes, smoked salmon, bagels, cream cheese, fruit, and more! I would really challenge you to make this board using all store-bought ingredients, this is meant to inspire you on how to showcase your goodies without stressing out.

Prep: 10-15 min. | **Cook: 0 min.** | **Ready In: 10-15 min.** | **Serves: 8–12**

INGREDIENTS

On a board it's always good to try and get a variety of items. If you don't like something on my board, substitute it for something else. Better yet, ask the bride for a list of her favorite items and swap things in and out. See my charcuterie board Pro Tip below!

SAVORY ITEMS TO INCLUDE:
(I find people gravitate to the savory items)

Smoked salmon and capers, avocados and veggies, eggs cooked how you want (hard-boiled or scrambled), burrata and roasted tomatoes, roasted potatoes, bacon

BREADS TO INCLUDE:

Naan, biscuits, bagels

SWEETS TO INCLUDE:

fruit, donut holes, powdered donuts, 2–3 different types of cream cheese

GREENS TO INCLUDE:

6 sprigs dill, 3 sprigs basil, arugula, or wilted spinach

INSTRUCTIONS

1. Arrange everything on your board and let everyone dig in and pile food on their own plates.

PRO TIP:
Different-sized bowls that are different heights will add personality and help promote visual interest in your board!

ZESTY LEMON DIP WITH FRUIT

I grew up attending bridal showers in the fellowship hall at my church. I loved watching women in pretty sundresses sip from their teacups and eat fresh fruit dipped in cream cheese. Things have evolved quite a bit from the days in Fellowship Hall, and one of my favorite things about creating recipes is taking something nostalgic and putting a twist on it. This dip isn't just for a bridal brunch; it can be for an easy Saturday morning with the girls or a Tuesday evening reality show party. Regardless of the moment, this dip is super sweet and encourages sweet conversation.

Prep: 5 min. | **Cook: 0 min.** | **Ready In: 5 min.** | **Serves: 10–12**

INGREDIENTS

½ cup cream cheese, softened

½ cup lemon curd

¼ cup powdered sugar

INSTRUCTIONS

1. In a medium bowl, mix everything together.

2. Serve with strawberries.

NO-BAKE FRUIT CHEESECAKE

That veggie tray at the grocery store sounds a lot easier and faster than making something at home. "You don't have enough time," you tell yourself. Not true! Almost every recipe in this book can be made in less than an hour, most in 30 minutes or less. But this recipe is beyond easy. It takes something plain from the store and dresses it up a little! So when you're tempted to say, "I don't have time for this," I would challenge you to change your way of thinking and respond instead by saying, "Yes, I'm busy, but God calls me to serve, so I can do this!"

Prep: 5 min. | **Cook: 0 min.** | **Ready In: 5 min.** | **Serves: 10–12**

INGREDIENTS

1 plain cheesecake (yes, I said it—go ahead and buy the store-bought plain cheesecake!)

¼ cup mixed berry jam

1 cup fresh blueberries

1 cup blackberries

1 cup strawberries, chopped

1 cup raspberries

Zest of 1 lemon

Mint sprigs

6 pansies (flowers)

INSTRUCTIONS

1. Take mixed berry jam and brush a little on 4 slices. On top of those slices layer alternate blueberries and blackberries. See picture for inspiration.

2. On the remainder of the slices, take the cut strawberries and raspberries and alternate.

3. Garnish the blueberries with lemon zest and the strawberries and blackberries with mint leaves.

4. Place the pansies for a pop of personality!

TABLE TALK WITH ABBY

As I was writing this book, the two questions I was asked the most were (1) What's your favorite recipe? and (2) What's your favorite section in the book? I must say, this might be my favorite chapter, and I hope it is used the most. Why do I say that? If your community is anything like mine, there are a lot of opportunities to serve in moments of celebration, mourning, and enjoyment.

There are exciting moments that happen when you want a festive drink and a fun appetizer. But then there are other moments when you aren't quite sure what to say; you don't have solutions or the answers. You just have love. God-centered love is put on display when we serve others no matter what the moment. God calls us to be obedient, show up, and serve.

TURKEY TACO QUINOA SKILLET

Meal trains are so wonderful. Whether a family is transitioning to a unit of three or four or five, it is so nice for them not to have to worry about meals for the first few weeks. And a meal train is a really tangible way for your community of friends to support, pray for, and love on each other. I love this skillet because not only will a family have leftovers for days, but it's a healthy alternative to a beloved meal that kids and adults will both enjoy. There is a joy that comes with knowing someone took time to make you a meal and then brought it over, and all you have to do is open and eat. Note: After dropping off the meal, don't linger; sometimes all that is needed (or wanted) is the front porch drop-off. You can walk away knowing this recipe is a winner!

Prep: 20 min. | **Cook: 60 min.** | **Ready In: 80 min.** | **Serves: 8–10**

INGREDIENTS

½ cup yellow onion, diced

½ pound lean ground turkey

2 tablespoons garlic paste

1 teaspoon chili powder

½ teaspoon cumin

1 4-ounce can diced green chilies, drained and patted dry

1 15-ounce can black beans, drained and rinsed

½ cup canned corn

1 14.5-ounce can diced fire-roasted tomatoes

1 cup salsa

½ cup rinsed quinoa

½ cup water

½ cup shredded Monterey Jack cheese

½ cup shredded cheddar cheese

Cilantro for garnish

INSTRUCTIONS

1. Heat a large skillet or cast-iron skillet over medium-high heat and grease with cooking spray or olive oil.

2. Add the diced onion and cook until translucent. Add the ground turkey and minced garlic and cook until the meat is cooked through (make sure to crumble the meat as it cooks).

3. Stir in all the spices, diced green chilies, black beans, corn, tomatoes, salsa, and quinoa until everything is combined.

4. Add the water in 3 parts while stirring. Put the lid over the skillet and cook on low-medium heat for 20 minutes until the quinoa is cooked. You want to cook it so the quinoa isn't hard and crunchy.

5. At this point, if you are taking this as a food gift, move the mixture to a take-out container. If you will be serving it out of the skillet, continue with the next step.

6. Sprinkle the cheese on top and cover with the lid, cooking until the cheese is melted. If you have moved your mixture to a take-out container, you can add the cheese to the mixture, or take the shredded cheese with you so your friends can add it when they are ready to eat it.

7. Serve as is, in tacos, or in a taco salad!

CROQUE MONSIEUR CASSEROLE

Comfort food—that is exactly what your friends need during sleepless nights—and days—with a newborn. Casseroles are also a great option when trying to figure out what to take to the new mommy's home. You can usually make them in a single-use container, and they can often be reheated and enjoyed for several days. Croque Monsieur is just French for "hot ham and cheese sandwich." All this recipe does is take ham and cheese sandwiches and turn them into a yummy casserole. Is your mouth watering yet?

Prep: 20 min. | **Cook: 40 min.** | **Ready In: 60 min.** | **Serves: 12**

INGREDIENTS

½ pound diced ham

½ pound deli ham

1 loaf French bread, cut into chunks

2 cups Gouda cheese, shredded

1 cup Monterey Jack cheese, shredded

8 large eggs

1 cup milk

1½ cups half-and-half

2 tablespoons Dijon mustard

1 teaspoon salt

1 teaspoon black pepper

4 sprigs fresh thyme, chopped

½ cup unsalted butter, melted

INSTRUCTIONS

1. Preheat oven to 375 degrees F and grease a 9x11 baking dish.

2. On the stove, sauté ham in skillet over medium-high heat to char the ends. This brings the fat in the ham to the surface and will make your casserole more flavorful.

3. In a large bowl add the bread, cheeses, and ham.

4. In a separate bowl whisk eggs, milk, half-and-half, mustard, salt, pepper, thyme, and cooled melted butter. You want to avoid the hot butter cooking any of the eggs.

5. Pour egg mixture over bread mixture and put in baking dish. Cover with foil.

6. Bake 30 minutes, covered, and then remove foil for remaining 10 minutes until the tops get brown and fluffy.

APPLE PIE BITES

Life changes are such a sweet part of growing up, and they are some of the sweetest moments for friends to share together. In fact, Jesus loved celebrating moments with people, and we are called to do the same thing. In Psalm 30:11–12 David says, "You [God] have...clothed me with joy, that I might sing praises to You" (NLT). Let us sing praises to God by serving those around us with the sweetness of food.

Prep: 10 min. | **Cook: 15 min.** | **Ready In: 25 min.** | **Serves: 10–12**

INGREDIENTS

1 can refrigerated crescent roll dough

2 peeled and sliced apples (grocery stores will sometimes have this already done for you; since these are not being served fresh, take the shortcut!)

½ cup butter, cut into 16 pieces

¼ cup butter, melted

½ cup sugar

¼ cup brown sugar

3 tablespoons cinnamon

INSTRUCTIONS

1. Preheat the oven to 375 degrees F and grease a cookie sheet.

2. Unroll the crescent rolls and separate.

3. Mix brown sugar, sugar, and cinnamon in a bowl.

4. Place one pat of butter on each roll and sprinkle with sugar mixture.

5. Wrap one apple slice into each crescent roll and place in baking dish.

6. Top with melted butter and more sugar mixture.

7. Bake for 12–15 minutes in oven.

8. Remove and arrange in a cute basket.

NOTE: The amount of butter and sugar you put on top of the rolls will determine how brown and crispy they get.

SPINACH AND FETA QUICHE WITH SWEET POTATO CRUST

When I start to plan to take a meal to a family with a new baby, a couple of things go through my mind. First off, I consider what type of meal they want—breakfast, snack, dinner, dessert, or maybe they've requested something uber-specific. Next, I try to think about healthy versus comfort or sweet versus savory. The majority of the time I land on some type of dinner or breakfast casserole that can be categorized as comfort food. Then there are other times when I make this spinach and feta quiche. It's perfect for breakfast (or really anytime) and has a healthier, but still widely popular, crust made with sweet potatoes. It's a great twist on a solid favorite and an easy meal to share with people.

Prep: 20 min. | Cook: 60 min. | Ready In: 80 min. | Serves: 8–10

INGREDIENTS

CRUST:

3½ cups shredded sweet potatoes

2 teaspoons olive oil

1 egg white

1 tablespoon flour

1 teaspoon kosher salt

½ teaspoon black pepper

FILLING:

1 cup diced ham

2 green onions, finely sliced

2½ cups baby spinach

¾ cup low-fat milk

4 eggs

3 egg whites

1 cup Gruyère cheese

½ cup shredded sharp cheddar cheese

1 teaspoon salt

1 teaspoon pepper

INSTRUCTIONS

1. Preheat oven to 425 degrees F and grease a pie pan.

2. Drain and pat dry the shredded sweet potatoes. Place in a bowl with oil, egg white, flour, salt, and pepper. Mix well.

3. Put the mixture in the pie pan and distribute evenly. Pack tightly.

4. Bake for 20–25 minutes until golden.

5. Reduce the oven temperature to 375 degrees F.

6. Sauté ham and green onions until fragrant and charred. Add spinach and wilt.

7. Combine the remaining ingredients (milk, eggs, cheese, salt, and pepper), reserving ¼ cup of the Gruyère for later.

8. Put filling in the baked pie crust and top with the reserved ¼ cup cheese.

9. Bake for 35–40 minutes until eggs have set and top is golden.

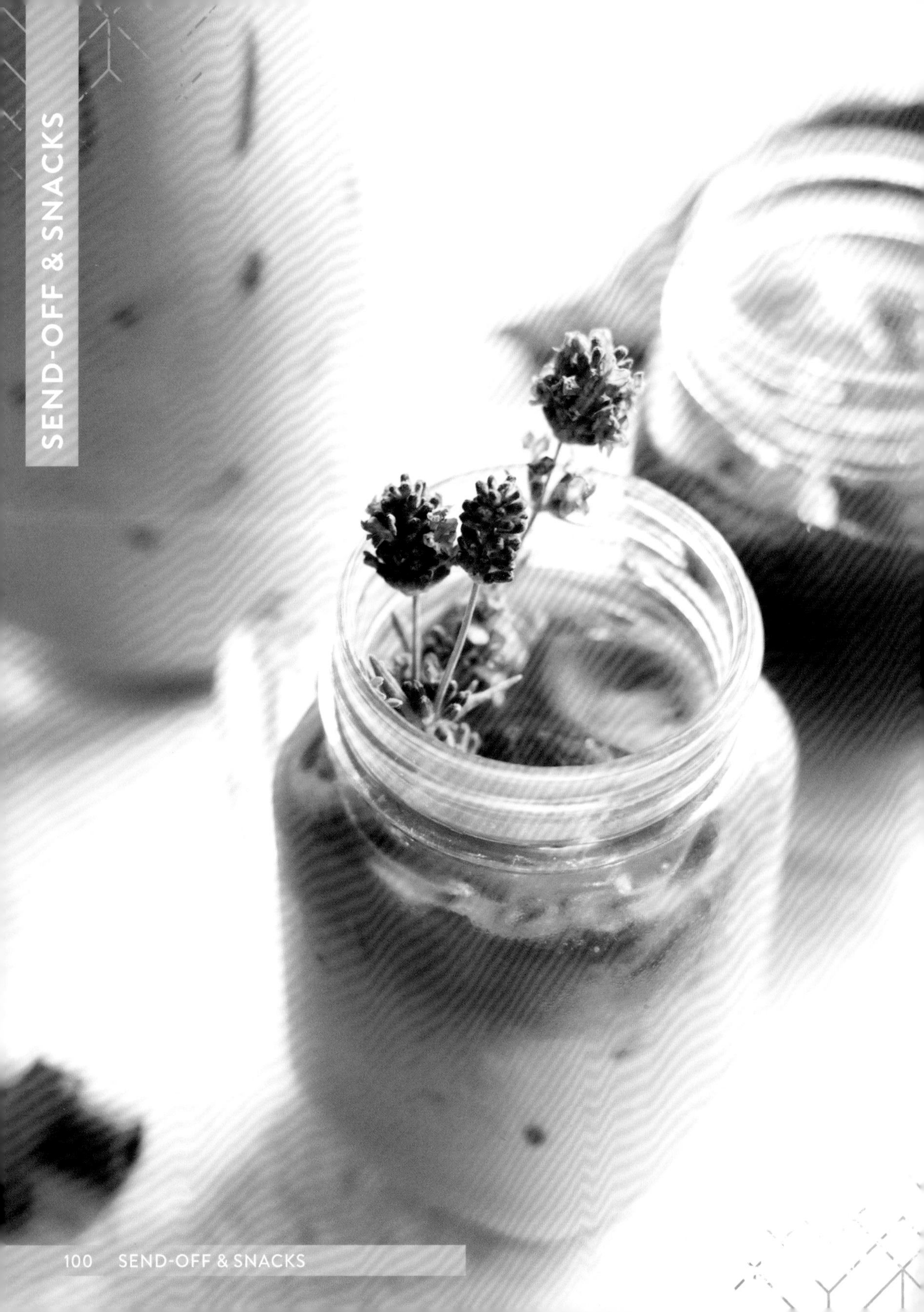

LAVENDER COFFEE PUNCH

Just like there are moments in life when we welcome new friends into our lives, there are also moments in life when we pray for the next chapter in someone's journey. Maybe it's a coworker who's accepted another job, a neighbor who is moving across town, or a friend who decides to backpack in Europe for a year. No matter the situation, taking steps into a new chapter can be exciting, but it can also be overwhelming and scary. During these times, it's important for us to remind our friends that God is with them. Deuteronomy 31:8 tells us, "He will be with you; he will not leave you or forsake you. Do not fear or be dismayed" (ESV). After reminding your friends of God's presence with them, be sure to send them off with a goodbye coffee!

Prep: 5 min. | Cook: 15 min.
Ready In: 15 min. + enough time to chill | Serves: 10–12

INGREDIENTS

2 cups half-and-half

¼ cup sugar or sweetener of choice

1 tablespoon vanilla extract

½ teaspoon ground cinnamon

½ cup dried culinary lavender (can be found at specialty grocery stores in spice section)

6 cups iced coffee

INSTRUCTIONS

1. In a saucepan, bring half-and-half, sugar, vanilla, cinnamon, and lavender to a boil and whisk. Boil 30 seconds. Simmer for 10 minutes. Note: you can also sub ½ cup of dried culinary lavender with 2 tablespoons lavender extract.

2. Strain lavender from milk mixture and combine in pitcher with iced coffee.

3. Drink immediately with ice, or chill in fridge until ready to drink.

RO TIP:
ake some into ice cubes by pouring the mixture into an ice mold.
at way you can put ice in the glasses without fear of the ice melting
d diluting the coffee.

MOCHA MOUSSE

We need to show up for people. I pray that you are using these recipes to not only connect with people but also be intentional about showing up for them every day. This mocha mousse is so easy to make. And, it is a great, sweet treat with coffee, perfect for an impromptu prayer visit with a friend.

Prep: 5 min. | Cook: 10 min. | Ready In: 15-20 min. | Serves: 12–16

INGREDIENTS

1 5.9-ounce instant pudding box

3 cups cold milk

¼ cup instant coffee granules

2 cups crushed chocolate sandwich cookies

8 tablespoons butter, melted

1 8-ounce container Cool Whip™

Fruit, if desired (I recommend strawberries and/or raspberries)

INSTRUCTIONS

1. Beat instant pudding mix, cold milk, and instant coffee together in a bowl. When combined and smooth, place in fridge to set for 5–8 minutes.

2. Mix 2 cups crushed sandwich cookies and 8 tablespoons melted butter together.

3. Press into the bottom of each serving cup.

4. Remove pudding from fridge and lightly fold in cool whip. Note: The fewer strokes you whip between the pudding and cool whip, the more color streaks you will have (see picture for examples).

5. Spoon pudding mixture on top of cookie mixture in each serving cups. Top with fruit, if desired.

PUMPERNICKEL AND POMEGRANATE BREAKFAST BITES

Saying goodbye to a friend can be hard, especially if she is a part of your tribe and her family feels like your family. One of the best ways to show love is to celebrate the moment with her. We will all go through phases of life where it is hard to celebrate. But we know our God is a God of details, and He knows every move we are going to make. I included this recipe because it reminds me of a traditional rye bread breakfast bite my mom used to make me. It takes a comfort food from memories I have and jazzes it up with some honey goat cheese. It's an easy snack that you can take anytime you need something tasty to serve to friends.

Prep: 15 min. | **Cook: 0 min.** | **Ready In: 15 min.** | **Serves: 16**

INGREDIENTS

6 ounces soft goat cheese

¼ cup cream cheese

1 tablespoon heavy whipping cream

2 tablespoons honey

2 tablespoons fresh thyme leaves, finely minced

16 slices pumpernickel or rye bread, toasted

½ cup pomegranate seeds, rinsed and patted dry

¼ cup finely chopped candied pecans

INSTRUCTIONS

1. Whip the goat cheese, cream cheese, heavy whipping cream, honey, and fresh thyme together in a mixer until light and fluffy for about 3 minutes.

2. Spread bread slices with cheese and sprinkle with pomegranates and candied pecans. Top with leftover thyme.

3. Enjoy!

AVOCADO TOAST BAR

Time spent with friends is never wasted. God is faithful in every moment we spend loving others by serving them. When we serve people, we are quite literally building up the kingdom of God. Sometimes these moments come out of nowhere and you don't have time to prepare anything. This avocado board can be easily made with ingredients you have on hand. I put examples of what you can add to your board below, but get creative! It's more about spending time with others than it is about having the perfect spread.

Prep: 15 min. | **Cook: 10 min.** | **Ready In: 25 min.** | **Serves: 8–10**

INGREDIENTS

8 avocados

2 lemons, juiced

2 teaspoons salt and pepper (this is more to taste—I like my avocado spread salty)

2 loaves French bread, sliced in ½-inch pieces and toasted

SPREAD EXAMPLES—GET CREATIVE WITH THESE!

Chia seeds

Sliced hard-boiled eggs (you can buy hard-boiled eggs from the grocery store)

Feta cheese

Cherry tomatoes, halved

Cucumbers

Radishes

Olives

Nuts

Capers

Smoked salmon

Sprouts

Jam

Ricotta cheese

INSTRUCTIONS

1. Mash avocados and mix in lemon juice, salt, and pepper. I like to keep my avocado spread pretty chunky.

2. Pick between 5–8 ingredients for your spread and put out in bowls or on a platter. (You know how I feel about charcuterie boards, so that's how I do mine!)

3. While you are encouraging your friends, let everyone get a plate and make their own toast!

NOTE: I tend to use 2 avocados for every 3 people. You can adjust the ingredients as needed.

BREAKFAST SAUSAGE BUNDT CAKE

Have a new neighbor? One of my very favorite moments is surprising a new neighbor with a welcoming treat. I love getting new neighbors—I'm constantly keeping my eyes open for moving vans and brown boxes in yards. Why do I love bringing goodies to strangers? Because that means I can potentially have a new friend in my tribe—a new person to intentionally love. This is my go-to recipe when it comes to new neighbors because let's face it, there aren't many people who would dislike a breakfast sausage Bundt cake.

Prep: 15 min. | **Cook: 30 min.** | **Ready In: 45 min.** | **Serves: 10–12**

INGREDIENTS

5 ounces breakfast sausage

Pinch of black pepper

1 teaspoon salt

1 teaspoon garlic powder

2 16.3-ounce packages large refrigerated breakfast biscuits

8 tablespoons unsalted butter, divided in half

8 ounces shredded Colby Jack cheese

1 tablespoon chopped fresh chives

INSTRUCTIONS

1. Preheat oven to 350 degrees F. Grease Bundt pan.

2. In a skillet, cook breakfast sausage three-fourths of the way through with pepper and salt and garlic powder.

3. Quarter each biscuit and put in a large bowl.

4. Pour 8 tablespoons of melted butter over the biscuits and stir to incorporate.

5. Sprinkle in sausage and half of the cheese. Mix well.

6. As you pour the biscuit mixture into the Bundt pan, layer in remaining cheese throughout.

7. Cover with foil and bake for 30 minutes until cooked through.

8. Invert onto a plate and serve with a smile!

RO TIP:
he oven will finish cooking the sausage; the longer you cook the usage in the skillet, the more cooked it will be in the oven. I like rving it upside down so you can see the pull-apart pieces better!

CHEESY BROCCOLI QUINOA CASSEROLE

Do you ever feel like you are all alone in the world? Like no one is investing in you? Maybe you doubt God is even there. Friend, God is there even when you feel alone. Before He left His friends (aka the disciples) and ascended into heaven, He told them to "go...and make disciples" (Matthew 28:19 ESV). He was telling them to go out and find people and love them. Don't let doubts cloud your mind. Instead, ask God to clearly show you who He wants you to share life with, who needs to hear His message of love the most, and whose life you need to impact. And then follow through! This recipe is a great housewarming treat and a surefire way to open the door for conversations with new friends.

Prep: 15 min. | Cook: 45 min. | Ready In: 60 min. | Serves: 8–10

INGREDIENTS

2 cups vegetable broth

1 cup quinoa, rinsed and drained

1½ cups shredded cheddar cheese

6 ounces freshly shredded Gouda cheese

1 cup low-fat milk

16 ounces broccoli florets

2 tablespoons olive oil

1 teaspoon salt

1 slice whole wheat bread

1 tablespoon butter, melted

2 tablespoons garlic salt

½ teaspoon pepper

INSTRUCTIONS

1. Preheat oven to 400 degrees F.

2. Bring the vegetable broth to a boil in a saucepan over the stove. Add the quinoa and reduce to a low-medium simmer. Cook uncovered until all the liquid has been absorbed by the quinoa (about 15 minutes).

3. Remove from heat. Add 1 ½ cups cheddar cheese and 1 cup Gouda to quinoa. Pour in milk and stir until milk and cheese are combined well with quinoa.

4. Toss broccoli in olive oil and salt and roast in air fryer or on greased sheet pan in oven at 400 degrees F for 20 minutes or until edges start to caramelize.

5. Make the bread crumbs by putting slice of bread and 1 tablespoon melted butter, garlic salt, and pepper in a food processor.

6. After broccoli is done, reduce oven to 350 degrees F.

7. Pour the cheesy quinoa into 9x11 baking dish and stir in roasted broccoli. Sprinkle with the rest of the cheese and bread crumbs.

8. Bake uncovered for 25 minutes until the top is golden brown.

9. Share with your new friends in the neighborhood!

MARINATED CHICKEN AND VEGGIE SALAD

God is constantly at work in our lives. We've all heard the saying, "The only thing that stays the same is change." Our phases of life ebb and flow, and sometimes our tribes change with the seasons. Friend, stay vigilant. Show God's love, make a new recipe, and share it with someone. We don't always know the details of why God brings people into our lives, but we can share His goodness with people around us—both new and old!

Prep: 20 min. | Cook: 20 min. | Ready In: 40 min. | Serves: 8–10

INGREDIENTS

1 cup chickpeas

1 cup Greek salad dressing, divided

3 small heads romaine lettuce

3 plum tomatoes, chopped

2 avocados, diced

1 cucumber, chopped

1 cup marinated artichoke hearts, chopped

2 cups feta cheese

½ cup sliced roasted red bell pepper

½ cup kalamata olives, halved

½ cup Italian parsley, finely chopped

¼ cup red onion, roasted and sliced

GRILLED CHICKEN FOR TOPPING:

1 pound boneless skinless chicken breasts

GRILLED CHICKEN MARINADE:

⅓ cup plain Greek yogurt

¼ cup olive oil

½ cup lemon juice

1 tablespoon garlic paste

2 tablespoons dried oregano

1 teaspoon onion powder

¼ teaspoon paprika

1 teaspoon kosher salt

½ teaspoon ground black pepper

INSTRUCTIONS

1. In a bowl toss together chickpeas and ½ cup Greek salad dressing. Cover and let marinate in fridge until ready to serve.

2. Mix all the chicken marinade ingredients in a bowl. Add raw chicken and three-fourths of the marinade in a gallon Ziploc™ bag and let sit in fridge for 15 minutes.

3. Remove chicken from Ziploc™ bag and toss the used marinade.

4. In a skillet on medium-high heat, grill the chicken until it reaches 165 degrees, about 15–20 minutes, basting with the remaining marinade as you go.

5. Assemble the salad in a large bowl or platter. Toss with the rest of chickpea and Greek salad dressing mixture.

6. Cut chicken into slices or dice it to your preference. Place on top of salad and serve with naan.

BERRY CRUMBLE PIE

This pie is a cross between my favorite blueberry muffin streusel topping and the juiciest pie filling ever. Your new neighbor will be an instant friend with this recipe, and it will be a conversation starter to help share God's love.

Prep: 15 min. | **Cook: 30 min.** | **Ready In: 45 min.** | **Serves: 10–12**

INGREDIENTS

1 pie crust (the crusts that come frozen in ready-to-serve foil pans are perfect for gifting)

BLUEBERRY FILLING:

⅔ cup granulated sugar

¼ cup brown sugar

3 tablespoons cornstarch

1 teaspoon cinnamon

1 lemon, juiced and zested

5 cups fresh blueberries, rinsed and dried

½ cup diced apples

FOR THE CRUMBLE TOPPING:

⅔ cup all-purpose flour

⅓ cup light brown sugar

2 teaspoons cinnamon

⅓ cup cold butter, cut into chunks

1 tablespoon granulated sugar

INSTRUCTIONS

1. Preheat oven to 375 degrees F.

2. If using an unbaked refrigerated pie crust, blind-bake according to packaging (about 20 minutes). To prevent the pie crust from bubbling up, use pie weights or prick holes with a fork in the bottom.

3. For the filling, mix together sugars, cornstarch, and cinnamon.

4. Gently toss in the blueberries and apples with the lemon juice.

5. For the crumble topping, combine the flour, brown sugar, cinnamon, butter, and granulated sugar in a food processor. Refrigerate until ready.

6. Pour blueberry mixture into pie crust and sprinkle with the lemon zest.

7. Top with crumble mixture.

8. Bake for 30 minutes with foil on, then remove foil for the remaining 20–30 minutes until pie is golden brown.

9. Take to your new friends...oh, and don't forget the ice cream!

THE TABLE THAT PARTIES

Jesus loved parties. He loved being around people, sharing a meal, and I can just imagine Him being the best storyteller in the group. He focused His efforts on bringing different people together and showing love. Revelation 19:6–9 tells us heaven will be like a wedding reception for all eternity.

When you enjoy being with other people, when you celebrate with others, it breaks down walls, builds communities, and deepens friendships. Before Jesus came and shifted the thinking on parties, the Pharisees didn't associate with these partygoers they called "sinners." But then Jesus came and radically changed everything. He partied with the tax collectors, kids, women, and "sinners." Jesus knew what was important—celebrating life with people. He opened the door and asked everyone to come in.

Jesus focused on celebrating moments and building relationships. If it was good enough for Jesus, it is good enough for me. But, do we host parties anymore? I'm not referring to a birthday party or a bridal shower. I'm talking about a pool party, a neighborhood block party—you know, those parties people threw in the "old days." The everyday get-together.

Today, we revert to our couches and TVs. Not only are we not throwing parties around the table, but we aren't even sitting together at the table. We crave connection with others, but instead of connecting with people, we connect with devices. Still, we wonder why we have fewer close friends than ever before. Our devices allow us to avoid human exchange and the potential vulnerability that follows.

Acts 2:46 says, "Day by day, attending the temple together and breaking bread in their homes, they received their food with glad and generous hearts" (ESV). Let me break this down for you. Luke, the writer of the book of Acts, was saying the followers of Jesus were hanging out and eating in their homes together day in, day out. Not only did this bring them closer together as a community, but it brought them closer to Jesus.

In order to fully embrace our community, we must understand that our connection to God requires complete vulnerability. Vulnerability opens the door for deep human connection.

In my world, to feed someone is to love them. The table has played a vital part in reaching nonbelievers throughout church history, and today it continues to play a role in fostering relationships. The table should be a place that is inviting, and open, and allows people to connect over conversation and shared experiences. Invite your friends, neighbors, coworkers—invite the sick, the wealthy, the poor, the widowed.

Maybe you're not sure where to start or how to invite people. Or you're thinking how hosting parties can be exhausting and intimidating, not to mention expensive. I get it. I remember the first time I invited a hodgepodge of people over to my house. It was an Easter lunch, and up until that point I had only invited maybe two to three people over at a time. I decided to invite people from church, work, and groups I was involved in. No one really knew anyone so I thought maybe eight would show up, given that it was Easter and I assumed most people would be celebrating with their families.

That was not the case.

That Easter Sunday, eighteen people crammed into my 1,200-square-foot apartment. We laid out the food on the TV chest and sat anywhere I could fit a seat. Not only did serving lift my soul, but the conversation that flowed within the walls of that apartment glorified God. It wasn't perfect, it wasn't spacious, and we ate from plastic containers that everyone brought and reheated in the microwave. But the conversation that happened over those plastic containers and card tables developed meaningful friendships and glorified God.

I was shocked so many people came that day. Shocked because nobody had ever mentioned they were alone or didn't have a tribe of people to celebrate with. As humans in this social media culture of living up to our highlight reels, we don't like to be vulnerable and tell people when we feel alone. But at the same time, we crave community—we were actually made for it.

Don't forget that God calls us to open our homes. In Romans 12:13 the apostle Paul encourages us to "share with the saints in their needs; pursue hospitality" (CSB). I love that version, because of the word "pursue." Merriam-Webster defines the word pursue like this: "to find or employ measures to accomplish." Paul is encouraging us to name hospitality as the goal we are pursuing. We must seek opportunities to show hospitality daily. God expects you to open your home and invite people in. Invite people who don't look like you or think like you. We read this verse and glaze over it and say, "Check! I am hospitable to my friends." But there is something special about inviting someone into your home whom you might not know deeply. It is truly one of the single greatest expressions of love and friendship. By inviting them in, and creating ways to

be hospitable, you might just change someone's life.

John 1:16 says, "Indeed, we have all received grace upon grace from His fullness" (CSB). This means God has set up a table of abundance for each of us! So, when we feel overwhelmed, overworked, inadequate, or intimidated by throwing a party, remember that nugget tucked in the first chapter of John. When we fail in our wisdom, our resources, and our own fleshly strength, we need to give it over to God. Because when we fail, He has all the power and the love available and can "pour on the blessings in astonishing ways so that [we're] ready for anything and everything, more than just ready to do what needs to be done" (2 Corinthians 9:8 The MESSAGE).

This chapter is full of recipes for different types of parties. It doesn't include elaborate hosting inspiration, just the everyday get-together. The recipes are meant to supplement what everyone else brings. People will pitch in, so let them! They want to be included and feel needed. Let's have a party—and make it a potluck!

OOD FOR THOUGHT:

ow are you going to reach out and build your community today with people who might not look or think like you? Your itation to dinner could ultimately be their invitation to heaven.

n you identify a group of people who need community? Maybe it's your neighborhood; maybe it's the widows group church. It might even be the group of women you heard at the water cooler talking about how they're struggling with fficulties in life. Can you invite them over? Can you throw a party and begin building relationships with them?

s there been a time in your life when you felt alone and isolated? Think back on who was there for you and how God ought you through that time. How can God use you like that in someone else's life?

TABLE TALK WITH ABBY

I love throwing a good party. And oftentimes I think I can do it by myself. But God does not want us to go through life doing things by ourselves. He wants us working together as a team. First Corinthians 12:14 says that the body is made up of many parts. The body of Christ is a team made up of many unique parts!

As you think about throwing a party, why not think about inviting your friends and making it a potluck? If God's goal of throwing a party is to build community, focus on the people. Don't get distracted from building relationships with people by trying to have the perfect food spread or the best decorations. The following pages are filled with recipes that are authentic and not pretentious; they focus more on the people than on the preparation. So have a party and...#makeitapotluck!

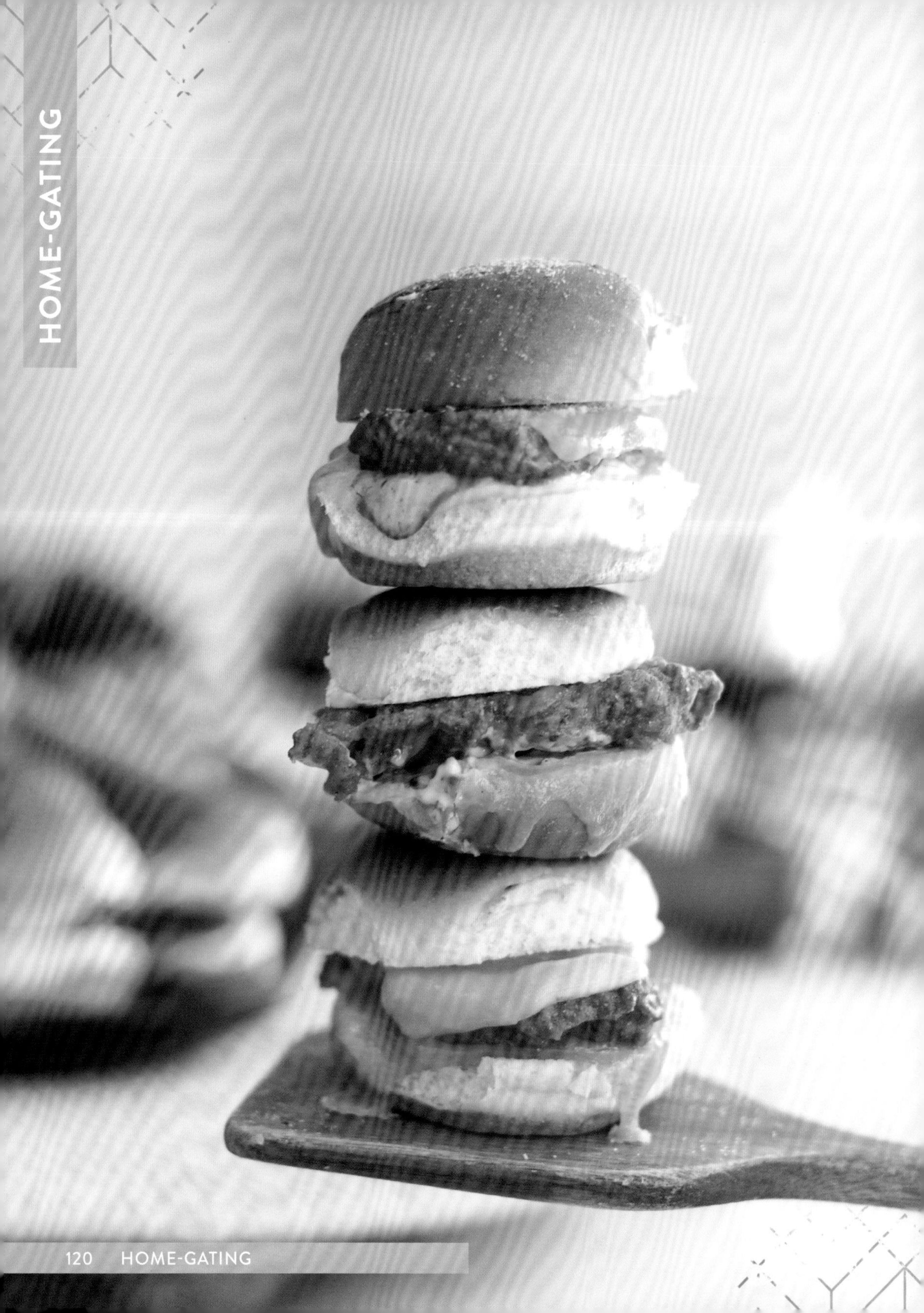

BUFFALO CHICKEN SLIDERS

One of the easiest parties to throw is to invite people over to watch a game. Most of the time the food gets gobbled up around the coffee table or off the kitchen island, and—trust me—as long as there is cheese and carbs, it is perfect game-watching food! Pick a game, invite your friends over, and #makeitapotluck.

Prep: 15 min. | **Cook: 20 min.** | **Ready In: 35 min.** | **Makes: 12 sliders**

INGREDIENTS

1 pound frozen breaded chicken tenders

1 cup buffalo wing sauce

12 Hawaiian rolls

6 slices cheddar cheese

¼ cup ranch dressing

6 slices provolone cheese

2 tablespoons butter, melted

1 tablespoon Italian seasoning

2 tablespoons Italian parsley, minced

INSTRUCTIONS

1. Preheat oven to 350 degrees F.

2. In a large bowl add chicken tenders and buffalo wing sauce and fully coat.

3. Cut the Hawaiian rolls in half, creating a top and bottom.

4. Place the cheddar cheese on the bottom, layered with ranch dressing, chicken, and then provolone cheese on top.

5. Place the top buns on the cheese.

6. Mix melted butter with Italian seasoning and parsley. Brush melted butter mixture over the tops of the buns.

7. Bake for 10 minutes.

8. Enjoy with your friends!

CREOLE SAUSAGE BITES WITH CREAMY CAJUN DIPPING SAUCE

Interesting fact: Did you know that the ESPY Awards show (sports award show on ESPN) is conducted on the Wednesday in July following the MLB All-Star Game because it is the only day of the year that there are no sporting events? Great news! There is a game on every day of the year except one day—and that's the day when we can watch the sports equivalent of the Oscars. This means there is never a day you can't celebrate sports. And there's never a day your friends won't enjoy these sausage bites!

Prep: 25 min. | **Cook: 20 min.** | **Ready In: 45 min.** | **Makes: 40 balls**

INGREDIENTS

1 8-ounce can crescent roll dough sheet

1 12-ounce package andouille sausage

2 tablespoons Creole seasoning

1 egg plus 1 tablespoon water for egg wash

CREAMY CAJUN DIPPING SAUCE:

½ cup mayonnaise

1 tablespoon coarse grain Dijon mustard

1 tablespoon ketchup

1 teaspoon Cajun seasoning

1 teaspoon fresh parsley, finely minced

2 teaspoons horseradish

1 teaspoon pickle juice

INSTRUCTIONS

1. For the dipping sauce: mix everything together and refrigerate until ready to use.

2. Preheat oven to 350 degrees F and grease a cookie sheet.

3. Unroll crescent roll dough, sprinkle with creole seasoning, and slice into ½-inch strips.

4. Cut sausage into 1-inch pieces and wrap with crescent roll dough.

5. Place on cooking sheet and brush with egg wash.

6. Bake for about 15 minutes until golden brown.

7. Serve with the creamy Cajun dipping sauce.

TAQUITO BOARD WITH DIPS

You heard at work that there is a big game on tonight. I hope your immediate reaction was "Come to my house!" If not, don't worry; we are learning the craft of hospitality together!

As I began to develop the confidence to have people in my home on a random evening, I had to move from the mindset of waiting for someone to invite me over to actually inviting people over. That can be super intimidating, especially if you don't think highly of your cooking or hosting ability. Don't worry—this board is perfect for an easy game night and comes together in minutes. So, if people are coming over for the big game, bookmark this page, run to the store, and enjoy this board with your friends!

Prep: 10 min. | **Cook: 20 min.** | **Ready In: 30 min.** | **Serves: 10–12**

INGREDIENTS

Taquitos—I like to do about 3 per person.(cook according to package)

3 dips—these are some of my favorites:

SOUR CREAM AVOCADO CREMA

2 avocados

½ cup sour cream

3 tablespoons extra virgin olive oil

4 tablespoons chopped cilantro

Juice of 1 lime

½ teaspoon chipotle chili seasoning

Salt and pepper to taste

FRESH GUACAMOLE

3 avocados

¼ teaspoon garlic powder

1 jalapeño, deseeded

¼ cup red onion, finely chopped

1 tomato, diced

3 tablespoons lime juice

Salt and pepper to taste

½ teaspoon paprika

½ teaspoon cumin

¼ cup cilantro, finely chopped

CILANTRO LIME RANCH

⅓ cup cilantro, finely minced

⅓ cup lime juice

1 teaspoon garlic

1 jalapeño, deseeded

1 packet ranch dressing mix

⅓ cup mayonnaise

⅓ cup milk

1 cup sour cream

INSTRUCTIONS

1. Blend each sauce's ingredients in a food processor and chill until ready to serve.

2. Arrange prepared taquitos and sauces on a board with fresh veggies and limes for garnish.

CREAMED CHICKEN BISCUIT BOWLS

There is something about Christmastime that just makes me want to host all the parties. A friend once told me, "Your house is my favorite during Christmas" (I think I might have cried a little on the inside). Thanks to Hallmark, we can celebrate Christmas starting November 1 with their Christmas movies—and celebrate again in July! These biscuit bowls are perfect for snuggling up on the couch with a warm blanket to watch your favorite feel-good movie. It's the perfect cold-weather comfort food!

Prep: 20 min. | Cook: 25 min. | Ready In: 45 min. | Serves: 8

INGREDIENTS

2 cans cream of chicken soup

1 12-ounce bag frozen mixed vegetables

½ teaspoon onion powder

½ teaspoon garlic powder

½ teaspoon salt

½ teaspoon ground mustard

2 cups shredded chicken

2 cans flaky biscuits

INSTRUCTIONS

1. Preheat oven to 400 degrees F and grease muffin tin.

2. Mix soup, vegetables, seasonings, and chicken in a bowl.

3. Press biscuits into muffin pan.

4. Spoon ⅓ cup of chicken mixture into each muffin cup.

5. Pinch the sides of the biscuit up around each muffin cup to hold mixture in place.

6. Bake 25–30 minutes until golden brown.

7. Serve with a warm blanket and the Christmas tree lights on!

FRENCH HOT CHOCOLATE BAR

I have shared a couple of French-inspired recipes that I picked up on my travels through France for my thirtieth birthday, but this one has to be one of my favorites. I had a drink similar to this at the little tea room at Château de Versailles. Marie Antoinette had a chocolate craftsman come to the palace and develop the recipe especially for her. They call it her "drinking chocolate." You really don't need the entire hot chocolate bar because this recipe stands on its own and is the perfect drink to cozy up with in front of the Christmas tree while watching a Hallmark movie!

Prep: 0 min. | **Cook: 15 min.** | **Ready In: 15 min.** | **Serves: 6–8**

INGREDIENTS

1¾ cups whole milk

½ cup heavy whipping cream

2 tablespoons brown sugar

½ teaspoon vanilla extract

8 ounces quality chocolate bar, semisweet (be picky—find a high-quality chocolate bar)

1 teaspoon espresso powder (optional, but it helps bring out the chocolate)

ADD-INS FOR HOT CHOCOLATE BAR:

Peppermint chips

Crushed Andes mints

Mini chocolate chips

Toffee bits

Whipped cream

Candy cane sticks

Marshmallows

Coarse sea salt

Cinnamon

INSTRUCTIONS

1. Simmer the milk, heavy whipping cream, brown sugar, and vanilla in a double boiler over medium-low heat.

2. Break the chocolate into pieces and place into the milk mixture (add espresso powder here, if desired).

3. Stir until the chocolate comes to a low simmer.

4. French drinking chocolate is considerably thicker than American hot chocolate. If it is too thin, simmer longer. If it is too thick, add ½ cup milk.

5. Serve with creative add-ins and cozy up with your friends.

NOTE: I like to make this hot chocolate using a double boiler. I learned that tip in the kitchen of Anne de la Forest. It's the authentic way to melt the drinking chocolate and avoid burning it.

REINDEER BITES

Not only are these perfect to munch on while watching a Christmas movie, but they are also great as party favors or as gifts for teachers and friends, and they're amazing to have around the house during the holidays! Did I mention they are super easy and quick to make?

Prep: 10 min. | **Cook: 5 min.** | **Ready In: 15 min.** | **Makes: 30 bites**

INGREDIENTS

30 mini candy bars

60 square pretzels

5 ounces vanilla melting chocolate

holiday sprinkles or crushed peppermint

INSTRUCTIONS

1. Line a baking sheet with parchment paper and top with square pretzels.

2. Put 1 mini candy bar on each pretzel.

3. Warm the oven to 300 degrees F; put the pretzels and chocolate in the oven for about 3 minutes.

4. Push 1 square pretzel down on each slightly melted chocolate.

5. Allow chocolate to harden

6. Melt the vanilla melting chocolate in a microwave-safe bowl for 30 seconds. Remove from microwave and give it a stir. Continue this process 30 seconds at a time until all melting chocolate is melted to avoid burning.

7. Dip one side of the pretzel sandwich into the melted vanilla coating.

8. Return to the parchment paper and shake sprinkles or crushed peppermint onto each sandwich before the chocolate cools.

CANDIED CHRISTMAS PECANS

For our holiday gatherings, my grandmother always makes candies with nuts. Now, I'm not normally a big fan of nuts; however, there's just something so nostalgic about a bowl of assorted nuts during the holidays. This is a great snack and even a great Christmas gift. Invite some friends over, tell them to bring their own party drink, snack on some pecans, and turn on tonight's Christmas movie.

Prep: 10 min. | **Cook: 8 min.** | **Ready In: 10 min.** | **Serves: 12–16**

INGREDIENTS

¼ cup bourbon

¼ cup brown sugar

2 teaspoons cinnamon

1 tablespoon granulated sugar

1 teaspoon salt

1 tablespoon unsalted butter, melted

4 cups pecans

Cinnamon and sugar for sprinkling

INSTRUCTIONS

1. Combine the bourbon, brown sugar, cinnamon, sugar, salt, and butter.

2. Add pecans and stir to coat.

3. Place the coated pecans in a skillet. Stir over medium-high heat until fragrant and caramelized, between 5 and 8 minutes.

4. While the pecans are still hot, toss in the reserved cinnamon and sugar.

5. Optional: Allow the pecans to set in oven on 175 degrees F for 30 minutes.

JALAPEÑO POPPER DIP WITH PORK RINDS

I'm always torn about food for tailgating. In Arkansas, it gets super hot during the first half of the football season and food can often spoil. This recipe is great no matter what the weather is. You can eat this dip warm or chilled, and it is super tasty!

Prep: 5 min. | **Cook: 25 min.** | **Ready In: 30 min.** | **Serves: 12–16**

INGREDIENTS

1 cup sour cream

8 ounces cream cheese, softened

2 cups shredded cheddar cheese

⅔ cup shredded Parmesan cheese

5 jalapeños, deseeded and diced

6 slices bacon, cooked and chopped

2 tablespoons Everything Bagel seasoning

TOPPING:

1 sleeve Ritz Crackers™, crushed

4 tablespoons butter, melted

1 package pork rinds for serving

INSTRUCTIONS

1. Preheat oven to 400 degrees F.

2. In a bowl mix the first 7 ingredients together.

3. In a separate bowl mix the Ritz Crackers™ and melted butter together.

4. Scoop the cheese mixture into an oven-safe dish and top with Ritz Crackers™ mixture.

5. Place dish in the oven and bake for 25–30 minutes until top is golden brown.

6. Serve with pork rinds!

NOTE: This can also be made in a slow cooker without topping with Ritz Crackers™.

BURRATA AND PEPPERONI WITH PESTO

I love a good tailgate party, only because it is usually a potluck and there is so much energy before a football game. I love this recipe because you literally throw it and go! I would suggest making it at the tailgate because it really is that easy. It is also a great way to keep the ingredients from mixing together or melting on a hot day.

Prep: 5 min. | **Cook: 0 min.** | **Ready In: 5 min.** | **Serves: 12–16**

INGREDIENTS

6 ounces sun-dried tomato pesto

8 ounces burrata

1 pint pepperoni, quartered and chopped

4 leaves basil for garnish

INSTRUCTIONS

1. Arrange tomato pesto on the bottom of a plate.

2. Top with burrata and sprinkle with pepperoni.

3. Garnish with basil .

4. Serve with toasted French bread and cheer on the team with your friends!

SOUTHWEST POTATO SALAD

Potato salad is one of those foods you can always find at a tailgate or BBQ. This recipe takes your basic potato salad and twists it all up so with every bite your friends will be wanting more! Invite your coworker or your neighbor to your tailgate or house for a BBQ—and make this. They will definitely want to come back!

Prep: 10 min. | **Cook: 20 min.**
Ready In: 30 min. | **Serves: 10–12**

INGREDIENTS

¾ cup ranch dressing

1 tablespoon lime juice

1½ teaspoons ground cumin

2 teaspoons ground coriander

¼ teaspoon chipotle chili seasoning

2 tablespoons butter

1 15-ounce can whole kernel sweet corn

1 poblano pepper, deseeded and chopped

2 pounds rainbow new potatoes, cooked and quartered

½ cup white onion, chopped

1¼ cups grape tomatoes, chopped

½ cup chopped fresh cilantro

Salt to taste

1 avocado, peeled and cubed

INSTRUCTIONS

1. Mix ranch dressing, lime juice, cumin, coriander, and chipotle chili seasoning until well blended.

2. Put 2 tablespoons of butter in a skillet on medium-high heat with the corn and chopped poblano pepper and let roast for 5 minutes.

3. In a medium bowl, mix the potatoes, corn, onion, tomatoes, pepper, and cilantro.

4. Drizzle the dressing over the mixture and toss to coat.

5. Season with salt and top with avocado.

6. Serve chilled and watch your friends devour it.

TOFFEE BARS

I love getting together with friends at tailgate parties, especially during September and October when the weather starts to get nice. I also like football games because I get to meet and talk with so many new and different people who are there to cheer on their favorite teams. God calls us to share His love with others. And sometimes if we love people through our actions first, it opens the door to deeper, more meaningful conversations later. Sharing these toffee bars with friends—new and old—will sweeten any conversation!

Prep: 10 min. | **Cook: 15 min.**
Rest: 30 min. | **Ready In: 55 min.** | **Serves: 20**

INGREDIENTS

2 sleeves graham crackers

1 cup unsalted butter

1 cup packed light brown sugar

1½ cups mini chocolate chips

1 teaspoon sea salt flakes

½ cup chopped pecans

½ cup Heath™ bar chips

INSTRUCTIONS

1. Preheat oven to 350 degrees F. Line a large baking sheet with parchment paper.

2. Place a single layer of graham crackers down on your baking sheet. It's best to use a cookie sheet with a lip.

3. Melt butter and brown sugar together over medium-high heat. Bring to a boil and then simmer for 4 minutes.

4. Pour entire mixture over graham crackers and bake for 8 minutes.

5. Remove from oven and sprinkle chocolate chips over the top, allowing them to melt for a minute or two. If needed, put back in oven for 3–4 minutes and spread chocolate with a spatula evenly.

6. While chocolate is still hot, sprinkle salt, pecans, and Heath™ bar chips on top.

7. Place in the freezer for 30 minutes. Remove pan from freezer and lift toffee out of pan by pulling up on the parchment paper.

8. With a sharp knife press into the chocolate to crack it into pieces.

9. Share with your friends!

CHEESECAKE SALAD

The healthier version of a cheesecake, this salad isn't really a salad at all. It's more like creamy goodness folded around some berries. Taste and see that the Lord is good, am I right?

Prep: 15 min. | **Cook: 5 min.** | **Ready In: 20 min.** | **Serves: 8–10**

INGREDIENTS

8 ounces cream cheese

½ cup + 2 tablespoons powdered sugar

½ teaspoon vanilla extract

¼ cup heavy whipping cream

8-ounces Cool Whip™

6 cups mixed fresh berries

Mint for garnish

INSTRUCTIONS

1. Beat cream cheese until completely smooth.

2. Add in the powdered sugar until combined.

3. Continue to beat as you add the vanilla and heavy cream.

4. Fold in the Cool Whip™.

5. Place the berries in the bowl and fold in gently.

6. Garnish with fresh berries and mint.

7. Enjoy with your friends on a hot summer day!

WATERMELON MINT PUNCH

Oh, the summer months and fun parties around the pool. Nothing quite like basking in the sun while getting to know your friends. What makes a pool party complete? A festive and refreshing punch!

Prep: 10 min. | **Cook: 0 min.** | **Ready In: 10 min.** | **Serves: 10–12**

INGREDIENTS

6 cups watermelon, cubed (usually about ½ a watermelon)

1 cup lemonade

¼ cup lime juice

½ cup mint leaves

2 tablespoons agave, can use honey as a substitution

Quartered limes for garnish

INSTRUCTIONS

1. Blend watermelon and lemonade together and put through fine meshed strainer.

2. Muddle (smash) lime, mint, and agave together and transfer to pitcher.

3. Pour the juice over the muddled mint and lime.

4. Serve over ice in a glass garnished with a lime quarter. Add sweetener if desired. Dive in!

PARTY CUBES

Drinking iced tea or lemonade around the pool is a must in the summer. Stay hydrated, right? Well, these fun ice cubes are perfect, and as they melt into your drink they add a burst of flavor! There's nothing like surprising your friends with this little trick. They won't see it coming.

Prep: 10 min. | Cook: 0 min.
Ready In: 3 hours | Makes: 24 cubes

INGREDIENTS

RASPBERRY MINT ICE CUBE INGREDIENTS:

1 cup raspberries

¼ cup mint leaves

1 cup water

LEMONADE ICE CUBE INGREDIENTS:

3 cups lemonade

Sliced cucumbers

Diced mango

Raspberries

Blueberries

Lemons

1 tablespoon sugar

INSTRUCTIONS

RASPBERRY MINT INSTRUCTIONS:

1. Blend raspberries and mint leaves until they are a paste.

2. Add water and mix together until well blended.

3. Pour into ice cube tray and add a few mint leaves for style.

4. Freeze for 3 hours.

5. Serve immediately after taking them out of the freezer!

6. Great for tea or lemonade.

LEMONADE INSTRUCTIONS:

1. Muddle 1½ cups fruit of choice individually with 2 tablespoons lemonade and a tablespoon of sugar.

2. Combine lemonade and muddled fruit.

3. Pour into ice cube tray and freeze!

BLT ROLL-UPS

No matter who we are or what we do, we are constantly influencing others. We influence our friends, our parents, our kids, our siblings, our spouses. Our words are the biggest tool we have. (Yes, even bigger than the food we feed our friends.) Use your influence to host a pool party, invite some new and old friends over, and enjoy these BLT roll-ups. What I love about these is that they fill you up but aren't over-the-top. They are "normal," and sometimes we just need a normal afternoon at the pool with our friends to let God move in big ways.

Prep: 10 min. | **Cook: 10 min.**
Rest: 10 min. | **Ready In: 20 min.** | **Serves: 8–10**

INGREDIENTS

6 spinach tortillas

2 tablespoons mayonnaise

1 head lettuce

12 strawberries, sliced

6 slices deli turkey

8 slices bacon, cooked

INSTRUCTIONS

1. Lay out the spinach tortillas on a flat surface.

2. Spread mayo first, then lettuce, strawberries, turkey, and 2 pieces of bacon.

3. Roll the tortilla tight. Pro Tip: Spreading enough mayo is crucial to getting the tortilla to stay wrapped tight.

4. Place in the freezer for 10 minutes to set.

5. Remove the tortilla from freezer, cut off ends, and then cut into ½-inch-wide rounds.

6. Eat these around the pool while chatting with your friends!

THE TABLE THAT WELCOMES

Jesus spent a lot of time around tables. In fact, one could argue that the majority of His mission was centered around people, food, and tables. Eating with people was His way of downloading the heavenly kingdom into the hearts and minds of the people He came to serve.

I am convinced that hospitality is one of the most important spiritual disciplines we can cultivate. Do you feel as if you're sitting on the sidelines, waiting for the perfect house? The perfect family? Or the perfect partner? If so, I'd like to encourage you to stop where you're at right now, take a look around you, and create time and space for a meal (at a table) with people you care about.

Let's take a look at how Jesus used the table in the Gospels. Jesus ate with Zacchaeus, a tax collector. The Jews despised tax collectors like Zacchaeus because Jewish tax collectors were hired by the Romans to take money from their fellow Jews. And not only that, but tax collectors were notorious for overcharging on taxes and keeping money for themselves. As far as the Jews were concerned tax collectors were traitors and thieves. While one would think Jesus would plan to eat dinner with the local pastor, the mayor, or anyone else respectable, He ate with the guy no one liked. What a perfect depiction of grace.

Do you think if someone had asked Zac if he was ready to have Jesus over to his house for dinner he would have said yes? Most likely, he would have said a resounding no with all sorts of excuses: "My house is wreck." "I don't have time to cook dinner." "The kids go to bed early." "It would totally mess up our routine."

It's uncomfortable to welcome people into your home—especially when they are unexpected. But the truth is, the journey toward true community requires us to take risks and embrace awkwardness. Yes, it is messy at times because God's children are imperfect people. But it is in those places of awkward discomfort that we can experience that same grace Zacchaeus experienced that day.

Being prepared to welcome people to your house on Sunday after church or Thursday night after the t-ball game is easy if you plan it out in advance. The recipes I have in this section are all about inviting people over and welcoming them into your home. Having paper plates and cups make easy to clean up and the great thing is, if you prep these meals and no one comes, the food won't go to waste. Eat the leftovers!

In 2 King 4:8-10, we read about a woman who Scripture refers to as "notable." She provided Elisha a place to stay and eat. It sounds like he stayed there often and she was always willing to open her home. Since they didn't have cell phones, I'm sure it was always unexpected. If you read on, 2 Kings 8:1-6 tells us that because she opened her home and served others, God continued to bless her.

It's not just food around a table—it's the literal breaking of bread, serving others, building relationships, and doing life together that leads to true community.

FOOD FOR THOUGHT:

Are you ready right now to open your home to someone? If not, what will it take for you to be ready? One part of being ready to welcome people into your home is the step you take to invite them in. Who can you invite into your home this week?

Sometimes it can be difficult to invite people into your home with children around, but what types of lessons would that teach them? How might your life, your kids' lives, your marriage, and your friendships be different if you lived a life full of inclusion and not exclusion?

BREAKFAST HASH

In the Hosting Handbook in the front of this book, I provide a list of foods to always keep on hand. This recipe is one that can be made with all frozen foods (except for the eggs), so it is a great breakfast recipe to use when you do have that unexpected guest. Maybe the guest stays a day longer. Part of building the discipline of hospitality is to be prepared. This recipe will help you be prepared when God gives you the unexpected. When God provides the unexpected, you can expect to be amazed at what He has planned.

Prep: 15 min. | **Cook: 10 min.** | **Ready In: 25 min.** | **Serves: 8–10**

INGREDIENTS

1 pound breakfast sausage

1 cup frozen diced potatoes, heated in microwave

1 tablespoon butter

½ cup frozen chopped green peppers, heated in microwave

Salt and pepper to taste

1 teaspoon garlic salt

½ teaspoon onion powder

½ cup shredded cheddar cheese

4 eggs

¼ cup Italian parsley, finely chopped

INSTRUCTIONS

1. Preheat oven to 400 degrees F.

2. Cook breakfast sausage in skillet over medium heat for 5–7 minutes, stirring often.

3. Heat the potatoes and peppers in the microwave and then put in skillet with 1 tablespoon butter, salt and pepper, garlic salt, and onion powder. Cook for 8–10 minutes.

4. Remove from heat and toss in shredded cheese.

5. Crack eggs on top of skillet and put in oven for 10 minutes.

6. Sprinkle fresh parsley on top and serve to your guests!

BALSAMIC GLAZED CHICKEN

This recipe has quite a few steps, but once you have cooked it once, it will quickly become a go-to recipe for you! Chicken is such a comfort food for so many people. I don't feel like you can go wrong with it. Your guests will be impressed and so thankful for this chicken cooked with goat cheese and caramelized balsamic glaze. Remember, you demonstrate your love for others when you open your home and cook for them.

Prep: 15 min. | **Cook: 15 min.** | **Ready In: 30 min.** | **Serves: 6-8**

INGREDIENTS

CHICKEN:

6 chicken breasts

6 ounces goat cheese

Salt and pepper

Garlic powder

1 tablespoon olive oil

BALSAMIC REDUCTION:

¼ cup shallots, minced

⅔ cup balsamic vinegar

2 tablespoons pomegranate juice

¼ cup chicken broth

¼ cup + 1 tablespoon brown sugar

1 teaspoon salt

½ cup pomegranate arils

¼ cup fresh basil, chopped

INSTRUCTIONS

1. Preheat oven to 350 degrees F.

2. Cut a pocket into each chicken breast. Stuff with goat cheese and ssprinkle with garlic powder, salt, and pepper.

3. In a large cast-iron skillet, heat 1 tablespoon olive oil over medium-high heat.

4. Cook the chicken breasts until lightly golden brown on each side. Transfer to a plate.

5. Over low-medium heat, cook shallots until soft in the cast-iron skillet.

6. Add vinegar, pomegranate juice, chicken broth, brown sugar, and salt.

7. Bring to a boil to caramelize the sauce.

8. Add the chicken back in the cast-iron skillet and move the skillet to the oven for 15–20 minutes until cooked through.

9. Drizzle remaining sauce over the chicken breasts. Top with pomegranate arils and chopped basil. Serve!

BRIE PESTO AND PEPPER JELLY SANDWICHES

Talk about a throw-and-go sandwich that will put your ham and cheese to shame. The combination of ingredients is interesting, but the flavor profile will leave you speechless. I hope you have an unexpected guest so you can make this recipe. Better yet, don't wait! We all need a moment to just sit and enjoy life. So, make this sandwich, sit down and enjoy it, and thank God for all of the people in your life.

Prep: 10 min. | **Cook: 10 min.** | **Ready In: 20 min.** | **Makes: 2 sandwiches**

INGREDIENTS

4 slices sourdough bread

2 tablespoons butter, melted

4 tablespoons basil pesto

5 ounces Brie cheese, rind removed and thinly sliced

4 tablespoons pepper jelly

INSTRUCTIONS

1. Heat a cast-iron skillet over medium heat.

2. Butter both sides of sourdough bread and grill.

3. Sandwich Brie cheese with the pepper jelly and pesto.

4. Put the tops on the sandwich until the cheese has melted.

5. Serve them to your friends before they get cold!

PRO TIP:
Strawberry jalapeño jam is so amazing on this sandwich!

RASPBERRY PUNCH

My friends know anytime they come to my house, this is my go-to drink. These are juices I always have in my house. The ginger ale and pineapple juice come in cans, so I keep those in the pantry. The frozen orange juice can stay in the freezer. And I drink raspberry lemonade like it is going out of style; it is always on my grocery list. No, you don't need a special drink when people come over. However, I challenge you to elevate your mindset. What if you were at someone's home and they made a special drink for you? You'd feel loved and noticed.

Prep: 5 min. | **Cook: 0 min.** | **Ready In: 5 hours** | **Serves: 8–10**

INGREDIENTS

RASPBERRY MINT ICE CUBE INGREDIENTS:

32 ounces raspberry lemonade

2 cups ginger ale

8 ounces pineapple juice

12 ounces frozen orange juice

INSTRUCTIONS

1. Pour everything into a pitcher and serve.

TABLE TALK WITH ABBY

The expression "I love to host people" is the biggest understatement for me. There are not many things I love more than having a full table and a stocked fridge. There are not many nights when my table isn't full of random people that come over to eat whatever leftovers I warmed up on the stove. I love the community it fosters and the conversations of the heart that are had around my table. It truly is encouraging and life-giving. The recipes you will find in the next few pages are easy and simple. Welcoming people into your home should not be stressful, and with a little train of the brain you will have some menu options down in no time to enjoy a full table and a full heart.

ONE-POT CHICKEN AND RICE

That step God is calling you to take? That dinner you are meant to cook, the couple at work you are being called to invest in, or the college girl who needs to talk—do it. Are you intimidated? Nervous? Maybe the thought of inviting someone fills you with doubt. Maybe you're thinking, "Everyone is too busy to get together." Don't let this lie win! Use this recipe to reach out to them. Take that step. You can do it scared, you can mess up the recipe, and you can do it while feeling inadequate. But that's when God moves.

Prep: 20 min. | Cook: 10 min. | Ready In: 30 min. | Serves: 6–8

INGREDIENTS

CHICKEN:

8 chicken tenders

⅓ cup plain Greek yogurt

¼ cup olive oil

½ cup lemon juice

1 tablespoon garlic paste

2 tablespoons dried oregano

1 teaspoon onion powder

¼ teaspoon paprika

1 teaspoon kosher salt

½ teaspoon ground black pepper

RICE:

2 tablespoons olive oil

1 small onion, finely diced

1 medium zucchini, quartered

Juice from 1 lemon

16 ounces instant jasmine Minute Rice, cooked

½ cup chopped Italian parsley, for garnish

½ cup feta cheese, for garnish

INSTRUCTIONS

1. Combine chicken and marinade ingredients and put in fridge for 15 minutes.

2. Add 2 tablespoons olive oil to a skillet over medium-high heat and cook chicken for 2–3 minutes on each side to caramelize.

3. Add onion, zucchini, and lemon juice and cook for 3 minutes until slightly browned.

4. Add cooked minute rice to skillet and incorporate flavors of cooked onion and zucchini.

5. Serve with fresh parsley and feta cheese.

ROTISSERIE CHICKEN FLATBREAD

Getting dinner on the table can be stressful, but I don't want it to be! Flatbread pizzas are some of the easiest dinners to make. You can even sub with a cauliflower crust to make it a bit healthier. This is a great recipe to add to your arsenal of meals, and I just love the BBQ on this one!

Prep: 10 min. | Cook: 10 min. | Ready In: 20 min. | Serves: 6

INGREDIENTS

2 cups rotisserie chicken, shredded

½ cup BBQ sauce

2 flatbread pizza crusts (I find mine in the frozen aisle; individual naan will work great too)

1 cup shredded mozzarella cheese

¼ cup sliced red onion

¼ cup finely chopped cilantro

INSTRUCTIONS

1. Preheat oven to 350 degrees F.

2. Toss the chicken in the BBQ sauce and spread the remaining sauce on top of the flatbreads.

3. Top each of the flatbreads with chicken, half the cheese, onion, and then finish with the remaining cheese.

4. Bake the flatbread on a sheet pan for 8–10 minutes, until the chicken is heated through and the cheese melts.

5. Top with cilantro, cut into strips, and eat dinner with everyone!

NOTE: I went to Kansas City with a friend several years back, and we ate at the restaurant Q39. I now dream about their chipotle BBQ sauce. They don't sell it, but man, when you find a good BBQ sauce, you keep it close!

PESTO PENNE

This veggie meal is great and uses only one pot, which is epic for dinner if you ask me! I didn't include any meat in this recipe; however, if you wanted to add some grilled chicken or even pulled rotisserie chicken, do it!

Prep: 10 min. | **Cook: 10 min.** | **Ready In: 20 min.** | **Serves: 6-8**

INGREDIENTS

16 ounces penne pasta

2 cups fresh baby spinach

½ cup cherry tomatoes, halved

⅓ cup shredded Parmesan cheese

⅔ cup prepared Italian salad dressing

½ cup basil pesto

Cracked black pepper and grated Parmesan cheese to taste

INSTRUCTIONS

1. Boil pasta for 10 minutes or until tender.

2. Add spinach, tomatoes, and Parmesan to a bowl.

3. Whisk the Italian salad dressing and pesto together and pour over the pasta.

4. Toss pasta with rest of ingredients. Top with cracked black pepper and grated Parmesan cheese as desired.

5. Serve with toasted sourdough bread.

CREAMY PARMESAN BASIL SHRIMP

You can't beat the combination of shrimp and risotto. I also really like to pair this risotto with scallops. Even though scallops take all of 2 minutes on each side to cook, I wanted to do something a bit more everyday friendly. This is the perfect meal to make after a day at work. It has cheese, carbs, and tasty shrimp, and your friends and family will love the creaminess!

Prep: 5 min. | Cook: 25 min. | Ready In: 30 min. | Serves: 6–8

INGREDIENTS

PARMESAN RISOTTO

2 tablespoons butter

2 tablespoons garlic paste

1 cup risotto

½ cup white wine

3 cups chicken broth

½ cup Parmesan cheese

SHRIMP:

1½ pounds large shrimp, deveined and peeled

2 tablespoons butter

¼ cup fresh basil leaves, chopped finely

1 green onion, roughly chopped

2 tablespoons garlic paste

4 tablespoons olive oil

2 tablespoons lemon and lime juice

1 teaspoon salt

½ teaspoon onion powder

1 teaspoon oregano

Pepper to taste

INSTRUCTIONS

RISOTTO INSTRUCTIONS:

1. In a large skillet melt 1 tablespoon of butter and garlic over medium heat until soft and fragrant.

2. Add the risotto and coat in mixture.

3. Add the white wine and the broth, ½ cup at a time. After each addition, wait until you get the mixture to a simmer before adding the next ½ cup. Stir frequently.

4. Cook for 20 minutes until risotto has absorbed the liquid.

5. Stir in 1 more tablespoon of butter and Parmesan cheese.

SHRIMP INSTRUCTIONS:

1. In a food processor, combine everything but the shrimp and the butter.

2. Pour the marinade over the shrimp in a large bowl. Let sit for 10 minutes.

3. Heat 2 tablespoons of butter in a skillet on medium-high heat.

4. Sauté for 3 minutes on each side (you should hear a sizzle).

5. Plate with risotto, squeeze a fresh lemon on top, and enjoy!

PINEAPPLE, MANGO, AND WATERMELON BRUSCHETTA

In Arkansas, summer movie nights outside are hard because of the bird-sized mosquitos we have. But I take this bruschetta with me to just about every outdoor summer event, whether it's at the pool, at the beach, or a backyard BBQ. The freshness is out of this world, and my friends love it. It's the perfect refreshing bite to keep the conversation going.

Prep: 15 min. | **Cook: 0 min.** | **Ready In: 15 min.** | **Serves: 8–10**

INGREDIENTS

SALSA:

½ seedless watermelon, finely diced

1 cup diced mango and pineapple

½ medium red onion, finely diced

⅓ cup mint leaves, finely minced

2 tablespoons honey

¼ cup lime juice

Salt to taste (I use 1½ teaspoons)

BRUSCHETTA:

1 cup ricotta cheese

French bread, cut into ½-inch-thick slices and toasted

INSTRUCTIONS

1. Mix all the salsa ingredients together.

2. Serve salsa atop ricotta cheese on French bread or serve straight out of the bowl with tortilla chips.

STRAWBERRY SHORTCAKE

These strawberry shortcakes should not wait for a movie night. They should be made as fast as you read this recipe. We like to get fresh strawberries from a local farm, and they are delicious on top of these homemade shortcakes. Invite your friends over during the summer for a back-porch evening chat and a tasty summer dessert! Even better, invite several friends over and decide on a rom-com to watch.

Prep: 10 min. | **Cook: 25 min.** | **Ready In: 35 min.** | **Serves: 8–10**

INGREDIENTS

2 cups flour

2 teaspoons baking powder

¼ teaspoon baking soda

⅔ cup sugar and 3 tablespoons sugar for strawberries

½ teaspoon salt

1½ cups heavy cream

1 teaspoon vanilla extract

3½ cups strawberries, sliced

2 cups whipped cream

INSTRUCTIONS

1. Preheat oven to 400 degrees F and grease an 8x8 baking dish.

2. In a stand mixer with pastry handle, combine flour, baking powder, baking soda, ⅔ cup sugar, and salt.

3. Blend in heavy cream and vanilla until mixture is stiff and not crumbly.

4. Move dough to greased 8x8 baking dish.

5. Bake 20–25 minutes or until a toothpick comes out clean.

6. Slice shortcake into squares or use a cookie cutter to create shapes

7. Toss chopped strawberries with 3 tablespoons sugar.

8. Top shortcake squares with whipped cream and strawberries.

CHEESY BACON CHIPS

What is better than a carb-filled chip to munch on during the movies? I could argue—nothing. I love these chips because they are easy and fast, and I never have leftovers. These chips are dangerous, and I love that my friends love them as much as I do!

Prep: 10 min. | **Cook: 20 min.** | **Ready In: 30 min.** | **Serves: 10–12**

INGREDIENTS

1 bag kettle-cooked sea salt potato chips

¼ cup brown sugar

¼ cup maple syrup

1 cup shredded cheddar cheese

10 slices bacon, cooked and crumbled

½ teaspoon paprika

¼ cup sour cream

INSTRUCTIONS

1. Preheat oven to 350 degrees F.

2. Spread the bag of chips onto a baking sheet lined with parchment paper.

3. Sprinkle brown sugar over the chips, then the maple syrup, and then the cheese and bacon.

4. Sprinkle on the paprika and bake for 10 minutes.

5. Remove and break the chips up.

6. Optional: serve with sour cream!

STRAWBERRY ORANGE JULIUS

The urgency of friendship in life is hard to comprehend. Time is not an unlimited resource. I look back over the last several years, and I wish I had made more friends—I wish I had reached more people with God's love. We only have so many moments in life, and it really does matters how we spend them. Summer Movie Nights (or fall movie nights if you are in the South) are a great way to love on people and deepen those relationship. This is such a great drink for a summer night on the back porch watching a movie with friends. Don't waste a moment, and for sure don't waste the opportunity to make this drink.

Prep: 10 min. | Cook: 0 min. | Ready In: 10 min. | Serves: 6–8

INGREDIENTS

12 ounces frozen orange juice concentrate

2 cups sliced strawberries

1½ cups milk

½ cup heavy whipping cream

⅓ cup granulated sugar

1 teaspoon vanilla extract

2 cups ice

INSTRUCTIONS

1. Add all ingredients to blender except for ice. Blend for about 20 seconds until smooth.

2. Add ice cubes and blend again until smooth.

3. Garnish with an orange slice and a fresh strawberry.

4. Enjoy the drink with your movie!

FRUIT WATERS

I hope that through reading this book you have been challenged to open your home in new and different ways. I don't know what God is calling you to do, but can I encourage you to keep being faithful to His plan and keep chasing after the community He longs for all of us to have?

Prep: 5 min. | **Cook: 0 min.** | **Ready In: 5 min.** | **Serves: 4–6**

INGREDIENTS

POMEGRANATE AND ROSEMARY WATER:

¼ cup pomegranate arils

4 sprigs fresh rosemary

STRAWBERRY AND BASIL WATER:

10 strawberries, halved

1 lemon, sliced thinly in rounds

Handful of basil

POM-BERRY WATER:

10 strawberries, halved

½ cup pomegranate arils

*Try subbing coconut water with this one.

LIME-BERRY MINT WATER:

1 cup blueberries, lightly mashed

1 lime, sliced thinly in rounds

8 sprigs of fresh mint

INSTRUCTIONS

1. Have fun with any of these combinations and add to 1 pitcher of water.

2. Serve over ice and have fun!

PULLED PORK PASTRY PUFFS

BBQs have always been really intimidating to me. As a single female living in an apartment, I don't have a grill and I'm not very good at barbecuing. However, I can buy BBQ and make it a little festive! It's not about having the Pinterest-perfect party; it's about having the party. And these pastry puffs are amazing and delicious and made with pre-cooked pork! If I can do it, you can. So have a BBQ and #makeitapotluck.

Prep: 5 min. | **Cook: 25 min.** | **Ready In: 30 min.** | **Serves: 8–10**

INGREDIENTS

¾ pound cooked pulled pork (yes, I purchase pre-cooked pulled pork at the grocery store)

¾ cup BBQ sauce

1½ cups shredded cheddar cheese

½ cup red onion, finely diced

1 sheet puff pastry dough

1 egg

1 teaspoon water

OPTIONAL:

2 tablespoons dry BBQ rub

INSTRUCTIONS

1. Mix pork, BBQ sauce, cheese, and red onion in a bowl.

2. Carefully unroll puff pastry sheet out onto parchment paper and cut into 6 equal rectangles.

3. Brush each rectangle with BBQ sauce.

4. Put the cooked pulled pork mixture down the middle of half of the puff pastry rectangles, followed by the shredded cheese and red onion. (For this step, I use the deli pulled pork from the grocery store. It heats in the microwave for 5 minutes and is super tasty.)

5. Place the other half of the puff pastry rectangles on top and crimp the edges to form a puff pastry pocket.

6. Combine egg and water and brush pastry with egg wash. Sprinkle the tops with a dash of BBQ dry rub.

7. Bake 20–25 minutes until golden brown.

8. Slice and serve and of course do it with friends.

NOTE: There are several brands that have pre-marinated pulled pork in the deli section of the store that work great for this recipe.

RIB TIPS WITH SAUCE

Believe it or not, when I created this recipe and first tested it on people, it was for a Christmas party. Yes, I made ribs in the middle of winter for a Christmas party as an appetizer. And they were devoured. My friends loved them; in fact, one friend asked for the recipe so she could take it to her family for Christmas! It's a really easy recipe, especially if you have an air fryer, and will help bring people together.

Prep: 10 min. | **Cook: 45 min.** | **Ready In: 55 min.** | **Serves: 10–12**

INGREDIENTS

SAUCE:

4 ounces cream cheese

4 ounces heavy cream

2 tablespoons butter

4 ounces crumbled blue cheese

2 green onions, finely chopped

RIB TIPS:

1 rack baby back ribs

2 tablespoons olive oil

½ cup BBQ dry rub

2 cups BBQ sauce

2 tablespoons liquid smoke

¼ cup brown sugar

INSTRUCTIONS

INSTRUCTIONS FOR SAUCE:

1. In saucepan on medium heat combine all ingredients and mix until creamy. Top with green onions.

INSTRUCTIONS FOR RIB TIPS:

1. Pat ribs dry and coat both sides with olive oil and dry rub.

2. Brush 1 cup of BBQ sauce on the ribs.

3. Drizzle liquid smoke on top of the ribs and place in air fryer for 20 minutes at 400 degrees F. Rotate after 10 minutes.

4. Take out of fryer. Remove meat from bones and chop into bite-size pieces.

5. Toss in remaining BBQ sauce and sprinkle with brown sugar.

6. Put back in air fryer for 10 minutes, tossing after 5 minutes.

7. Serve with sauce.

NOTE: You can also make this recipe in an oven. Place ribs in a closed foil boat and place on baking sheet. Cook at 425 for 30 minutes. Open foil boat once you remove the meat from the bone and toss in sauce and sugar. Cook for 20 minutes.

GRILLED CORN SALSA

We each have a choice. We can decide whether or not we are going to invite people into our homes. I suspect you picked up this book because you want to. If at this point you haven't invited someone over, I would venture to guess it's because you think you aren't good enough to host a BBQ. Sister, get that out of your head right now! Like I say about all my recipes, this recipe is easy and everyone will love it. I promise—you can't mess it up.

Prep: 5 min. | **Cook: 10 min.** | **Ready In: 15 min.** | **Serves: 6-8**

INGREDIENTS

2 15-ounce cans corn (or 3–4 ears of fresh corn)

2 tablespoons butter

1 tablespoon liquid smoke

2 teaspoons salt, divided

⅓ cup chopped red onions

1 cup halved cherry tomatoes

¼ cup chopped cilantro

¼ teaspoon cumin

¼ teaspoon paprika

Juice of 1 lime

INSTRUCTIONS

1. In a skillet over medium heat, cook corn in butter, liquid smoke, and 1 teaspoon salt.

2. Halfway through cooking the corn (about 5 minutes) add the red onion to the skillet.

3. Cook until you start to see caramelization on the kernels.

4. In a large bowl add corn, tomatoes, cilantro, onion, remaining salt, cumin, paprika, and lime juice.

5. Taste to make sure you don't need any more salt or lime juice.

6. Serve with warm tortilla chips or on top of a taco salad.

THE TABLE THAT CELEBRATES

"B e hospitable to one another without grumbling. As each one has received a gift, minister it to one another, as good stewards of the manifold grace of God" (I Peter 4:9–10 NKJV).

During the holidays, life can be stressful. But what if inviting people to dinner during this hectic time reminds them of the true meaning of Christmas? What if hosting a get-together (however stressful it may be) is the only introduction someone may have to Jesus this season? God will use your kindness and generosity in ways you can't imagine.

Proverbs 11:25 says, "The generous will prosper; those who refresh others will themselves be refreshed" (NLT). I don't know about you, but sometimes during the holidays, my cup feels empty and I need to feel refreshed.

I think back to a Friendsgiving I threw several years ago. I made a huge turkey with all of the fixings—it was a sight to behold. But I was exhausted. I had been cooking for days for this party (something I will NEVER encourage), and I had decorated my home with all the pumpkins and gourds I could find.

I was the Martha in the story—focused on the product and so distracted by what I was doing that I completely missed the people. At the end of the evening, there was no desire in me to clean the table or do the dishes. My heart craved the community. I remember thinking that I had missed three hours of community building because I was consumed with my own "perfection"—a perfection that is not attainable.

I looked up from sitting on the couch post-dinner, and several of my friends had cleaned the table and put the dishes away. They were in the middle of preparing leftovers for my guests to take with them. Yes, I have trained my community well; they know they will always leave with a container of leftovers!

Without being aware, I had tried to outperform God. He quickly reminded me: "I need you to love on My people."

Jesus's last meal on earth wasn't an ordinary meal; it was the celebration of Passover. And it wasn't just any bread He broke; it was the unleavened bread (matzah). You see, Passover was the first holiday ever given by God to the Jewish people. Jesus understood the need to celebrate important moments with community throughout life. And the best part? He has invited us to celebrate life with a loving God for eternity.

Ephesians 2:6 says, "God raised us up with Christ and seated us with Him in the heavenly realms in Christ Jesus" (NIV). Look at the word "seated"—the past-tense form of the verb. It's a specific verb and one that can be easily ignored. God has already given us a seat at His table. And this is a table where we belong, where we are recognized and loved, secure and redeemed. Isn't that incredible? Isn't it amazing? We have a loving Father who, no matter what, loves us and invites us to His table. How could we not want to invite others to experience His great love and care? We have a unique purpose to celebrate life with others and bring them to His table with us. And it's more than a purpose; it's an honor.

No matter how busy life can get or how intimidated we feel opening our homes, God will help us take one step at a time. I hope you use these simple recipes to celebrate God's goodness with those around you! When you begin filling every seat at the table, Jesus works in ways we can't fathom.

FOOD FOR THOUGHT:

Do you live your life as if you are already seated at the table with God?
Are you using your table as a mission field and loving every person the way Jesus loves them?
What does it look like to have people at your celebration this year? Whether you need to open up another table, celebrate a new holiday like Galentine's Day, or fill all the seats at the table you currently have, how can you love more people during your celebrations?

CHICKEN NUGGETS AND WAFFLES

Second Corinthians 5:17 reminds us, "If anyone is in Christ, he is a new creation. The old has passed away; behold, the new has come" (ESV). This verse makes me think of New Year's Eve, a day most people celebrate by kicking out the old and putting on the new. Celebrate with friends on this day. Invite them over and encourage them. It's a new year, so stay up late, eat chicken and waffles, and celebrate what God has done and what God has planned.

Prep: 10 min. | Cook: 15 min. | Ready In: 25 min. | Serves: 12–16

INGREDIENTS

12 chicken nuggets

Waffle batter for 12 waffles
(I love the "just add water" mixes)

1 tablespoon cinnamon

½ cup brown sugar

4 sticks butter, melted

2 cups maple syrup

INSTRUCTIONS

1. Slice each chicken nugget in half or in thirds to get relatively flat.

2. Mix cinnamon and brown sugar into waffle batter.

3. Place pieces of chicken on waffle iron and pour waffle batter around and on top.

4. Close waffle iron and bake until golden brown.

5. Cut waffle into strips, skewer with a popsicle stick, and dip.

6. Serve by dipping into melted butter and syrup!

RUGELACH NUTELLA ROLLS

I first enjoyed these chocolate rolls in Jerusalem when I visited several years ago. Rugelach, pronounced roo•guh•laak, is a Yiddish term meaning "little twists". They were everywhere in the marketplace. However, I was really surprised that they are originally a Jewish treat from Poland and are more traditionally eaten around Hanukkah. When I returned home from my trip, I decided to put my American, quick-and-easy spin on them. Using crescent rolls, these whip up in minutes and are so poppable you'll need to make several batches for your New Year's Eve party!

Prep: 5 min. | **Cook: 15 min.**
Ready In: 20 min. | **Serves: 10–12**

INGREDIENTS

1 can refrigerated crescent roll sheet

8 tablespoons Nutella spread

Powdered sugar for dusting

INSTRUCTIONS

1. Preheat oven to 350 degrees F.

2. Unroll the crescent roll dough and spread Nutella thinly across entire sheet, leaving ½ inch around the edges.

3. Roll from the short side (like you would cinnamon rolls).

4. Cut rolls every ½ to 1 inch and put them on a greased cookie sheet. Bake them for 10–12 minutes or until golden brown.

5. Sprinkle powdered sugar on top of each roll (optional).

BACON JAM AND PIMENTO CHEESE PUFF PASTRY CUPS

There is still time! Don't let the year end without inviting someone over. I love pimento cheese, and I eat way more of it than I would like to admit. My grandfather would make pimento cheese and mayo sandwiches on white bread. To remember him, I have taken a very old-fashioned sandwich and introduced it to the twenty-first century with bacon jam and puff pastry! I'd say it is a perfect treat for friends to enjoy while watching the ball drop, don't you think?

Prep: 5 min. | Cook: 10 min.
Ready In: 15 min. | Serves: 12

INGREDIENTS

2 boxes refrigerated puff pastry shells

8 ounces pimento cheese

8 ounces bacon jam

INSTRUCTIONS

1. Preheat oven to 400 degrees F.

2. Follow the baking instructions on the puff pastry shells' boxes.

3. Place the baked puff cups on a cooling rack and press the centers of the pastry shells to the bottom.

4. Use a spoon to fill each cup with pimento cheese. Top with bacon jam.

5. Enjoy these while building relationships with your friends!

POMEGRANATE MARSHMALLOWS

I am always looking for fun ways to spice up a place setting for a party. These marshmallows are a super fun way to do just that, and they are a simple way to make any NYE party festive!

Prep: 5 min. | **Cook: 10 min.** | **Ready In: 15 min.** | **Serves: 6–8**

INGREDIENTS

Powdered sugar for handling

½ cup pomegranate juice

14 grams unflavored gelatin (2 7-gram packets)

2¼ cups sugar

1 cup cane syrup

½ cup water

INSTRUCTIONS

1. Line a 6x6 or 8x8 baking pan with plastic wrap and then dust with powdered sugar. Set aside.

2. Pour the juice and gelatin powder in a stand mixer and mix with a spoon to allow all powder to be absorbed into the juice.

3. Put sugar, syrup, and water in saucepan over low heat, stirring until everything is melted. You want a clear liquid with no sugar granules remaining.

4. Boil liquid until it reaches 260 degrees F.

5. Remove from heat and let cool so it is no longer bubbling.

6. Turn on stand mixer to medium and slowly pour syrup in. Avoid any grainy lumps getting into the mixture.

7. Whisk on high for 5–10 minutes until it's the consistency of very stiff meringue.

8. With oiled spatula, scrape mixture into the prepared square baking pan. You might need to re-oil the spatula several times, but try and work fast to keep the mixture from stiffening.

9. Let it set for 2 hours, then invert onto surface dusted with powdered sugar.

10. Cut into cubes with oiled knife (this will prevent sticking). Toss cubes in powdered sugar.

PRO TIP:
The wetter the marshmallow, the stickier it gets. And homemade marshmallows don't dry! So to add edible gold foil, cut the side you want to foil and stick the edible gold foil to the sticky part of the marshmallow.

FIZZ AND POPSICLES

Facing life alone can be hard. God never intended for us to live alone. In the beginning of His love letter to us—the Bible—He created Eve because it was "not good for the man to be alone" (Genesis 2:18 NIV). This is why we must open up our homes, celebrate life with others, and build up our community with Scripture. Especially on days when we feel like we are doing life alone. Let God use others to encourage you, and take the initiative to encourage others. Do it! Pick up your phone, invite some girls over, and toss a popsicle in a glass of your favorite fruit juice.

Prep: 5 min. | Cook: 0 min. | Ready In: 5 min. | Serves: 8–10

INGREDIENTS

1 box any popsicles from your local grocery store

3–4 11.5-ounce bottles fruit juice (I personally like the individual 11.5-ounce bottles because I can buy 3–4 different flavors and won't have a ton left over)

2–3 cans ginger ale

INSTRUCTIONS

1. Put popsicle upside down in glass.

2. Top with fruit juice and a splash of ginger ale for the bubbles.

3. Garnish with fresh fruit (optional). Cheers to friendship!

PRO TIP:
Make it a fun DIY bar and have a lot of different types (and colors) of juices and different types of popsicles. It'll make for a fun treat!

FRENCH-DIPPED MADELEINES

While I was traveling in France, I had the opportunity to learn how to make French madeleines with a chef. It was a delightful experience. Madeleines are a French dessert, and you need a special mold for them.

Prep: 30 min. | Cook: 15 min. | Ready In: 1 hour | Serves: 12–14

INGREDIENTS

8 tablespoons + 3 tablespoons butter

1 cup all-purpose flour (reserve 1 tablespoon flour for dusting)

⅔ cup granulated sugar

2 large eggs

1 teaspoon vanilla

1 tablespoon lemon juice

1 tablespoon lemon zest, finely grated

Powdered sugar to garnish

1 teaspoon salt

TOPPING:

¾ cup powdered sugar

2 tablespoons rosé

3 tablespoons dried rose petals (or pink sprinkles)

2 tablespoons granulated sugar

INSTRUCTIONS

1. Preheat oven to 350 degrees F.

2. Melt 8 tablespoons butter over low heat until it gets slightly toasty brown. Scoop 3 non-melted tablespoons of butter into a small bowl and set aside.

3. Whisk together the flour and sugar and set aside.

4. In another bowl, whisk two eggs with vanilla, salt, lemon juice, and zest until frothy.

5. Add the egg mixture to the flour and stir until just combined. Add the 8 tablespoons of melted butter and continue to stir until well incorporated.

6. Cover the bowl with plastic wrap and rest in the fridge for 10–20 minutes (or freezer for half the time). You want all the ingredients to get to the same temperature so they bake at the same rate in the oven.

7. Brush the 3 tablespoons of butter onto the madeleine molds. Sprinkle the 1 tablespoon flour generously to coat each mold.

8. Remove the batter from the fridge and put 1 tablespoon of the batter in the bottom of each mold.

9. Place in oven for 13 minutes. After 8 minutes, rotate pans clockwise.

10. Remove and cool.

PRO TIP:

Most grocery stores sell Madeleines in their bakery. You can save some time by picking up store-bought Madeleines and skipping to step 11 on the next page!

11. Whisk together the powdered sugar and rosé until smooth and slightly runny.

12. Dip the corner of each madeleine into the rosé sugar mixture, then sprinkle a few rose petals on each cookie.

13. Set aside and cool on cooling rack until the glaze has set.

14. Enjoy with your gal pals!

NOTE: I added a lot of rose petals to some of these for the pictures. I would recommend only a sprinkling of rose petals for the perfect bite! Or don't use rose petals at all but try fun pink sprinkles!

HEART-SHAPED WAFFLES
WITH MEYER LEMON CREAM

I love that women created a holiday for partying with your gals! I mean, come on—how perfect is this party! It is everything we love most. Love, friendship, and a themed party! So get out your pink dress and invite your gal pals over for a fun brunch with this tasty Meyer lemon cream for your waffles.

Prep: 5 min. | **Cook: 5 min.** | **Ready In: 10 min.** | **Serves: 8–10**

INGREDIENTS

4 ounces cream cheese

1 tablespoon Meyer lemon juice + 1-2 teaspoons zest

⅓ cup heavy whipping cream

2 tablespoons honey

8–10 waffles, cooked and cut into hearts with a cookie cutter

INSTRUCTIONS

1. Whip the cream cheese and lemon juice together until smooth.

2. Add the heavy whipping cream and continue to whip until soft peaks form.

3. Add honey and lemon zest and combine.

4. Put it on top of the waffles and serve with strawberries.

SPARKLING RASPBERRY FLOAT

There are friends at work you still haven't invited over. Little secret: they are looking for friends, too! Galentine's is a great way to get to know new friends. #makeitpotluck. Invite a bunch of girls and scoop some tart and tasty sorbet into a glass and serve this fun and fizzy drink! God doesn't want us celebrating life alone—so start inviting people.

Prep: 5 min. | **Cook: 0 min.** | **Ready In: 5 min.** | **Serves: 8–10**

INGREDIENTS

1½ cups raspberry sorbet

3 cups orange juice

3 cans Sprite™ or ginger ale or flavored sparkling water (I find that Sprite™ has the most fizz)

Mint leaves and fresh raspberries, for garnish

INSTRUCTIONS

1. In your glass, place a couple scoops of sorbet.

2. Pour in orange juice until the glass is ⅔ full, then top with Sprite™ (or ginger ale or sparkling water).

3. Garnish with a sprig of mint and raspberries.

TABLE TALK WITH ABBY

I love a good holiday party! Give me a theme and I can go all out. Friendsgiving is one of my favorites, though, because I really enjoy kicking off the holiday season with friends and family around my table and in my home. The best part about Friendsgiving is that everyone gets to bring something and feel like they contributed. There is something special about serving others while allowing them to serve you

back. I have found it breeds better conversation and creates an easier environment to dig in and foster community. I hope these next few pages bring you inspiration so you can celebrate throughout the year with your community!

PEAR, PROSCIUTTO, AND HONEY BITES

The season of Thanksgiving is always a great one for me. I enjoy the beginning of party season and really like the mindset that it puts me in. Being reminded constantly of everything I'm thankful for and blessed with is humbling because it forces me to recognize the work God is doing in my life. Maybe that is the first topic of conversation while you are eating these bites with your friends. What work is God doing in your life, and how do you recognize it?

Prep: 5 min. | **Cook: 15 min.** | **Ready In: 20–25 min.** | **Makes: 16**

INGREDIENTS

1 can crescent rolls

1 pear, sliced thinly into 10–12 pieces

8 slices prosciutto

5 ounces Brie sliced into ⅛-inch slices

½ cup honey

1 tablespoon fresh thyme leaves

INSTRUCTIONS

1. Preheat oven to 400 degrees F.

2. Roll out the crescent roll sheet and cut into 8 squares. Cut each square into 2 triangles.

3. Place the triangles on a baking sheet and cook for 8–10 minutes.

4. Remove from the oven and layer in pear, prosciutto, Brie cheese, and finally honey (in that order).

5. Sprinkle thyme over each muffin, pop back in the oven for 2–3 minutes to let the Brie, melt, and enjoy!

BOURSIN AND ASPARAGUS TARTLET

It's not enough to be thankful. Thankfulness is an attitude of action, not of idleness. Thankful for your friendships? Serve them. Thankful for your community? Invite them over for Friendsgiving. When God is at the center of our thoughts, our actions follow. Invite your friends over, serve them, thank them for the part they play in your life, and serve this incredibly tasty tartlet. You won't be disappointed. Note: This is also a great snack for your midweek Bible study or any small-group get-together.

Prep: 10 min. | Cook: 15 min. | Ready In: 25 min. | Serves: 6–8

INGREDIENTS

1 sheet puff pastry

1 package Boursin cheese, room temperature or slightly melted

1 bunch asparagus, roasted if preferred

Egg wash, if desired (1 large egg beaten with 2 tablespoons water)

INSTRUCTIONS

1. Set oven to 350 degrees F.

2. On greased cookie sheet carefully lay out the puff pastry sheet (the more you touch it, the less it will rise).

3. Spread the Boursin cheese on the puff pastry, leaving a thumbprint-size border.

4. Lay the asparagus on the cheese.

5. If desired, spread an egg wash on the border of the puff pastry.

6. Bake in oven for 15–20 minutes.

7. Remove from oven, slice, and enjoy!

PUMPKIN HUMMUS

Of course it is pumpkin season, so why not make something with pumpkin! Hummus is already tasty, and with a little bit of pumpkin puree and chipotle chili, you will shock yourself with how good this is!

Note: You can buy plain hummus and start with Step 2 if you don't want to make the hummus.

Prep: 5 min. | Cook: 20 min.
Ready In: 25 min. | Serves: 10–12

INGREDIENTS

1 15-ounce can chickpeas, drained

2 teaspoons olive oil

2 tablespoons chipotle chilies in adobo (I like to scoop directly out of the can)

2 tablespoons lemon juice

¼ cup tahini

2 tablespoons minced garlic

1 teaspoon salt (I like a coarse salt)

1 15-ounce can pumpkin puree

2 tablespoons BBQ spice (I use a sweet chipotle BBQ seasoning)

1 tablespoon cinnamon

½ teaspoon smoked paprika, plus more to top

Roasted and salted pepitas (pumpkin seeds)

INSTRUCTIONS

1. Put the chickpeas, olive oil, chipotle chilies, lemon juice, tahini, garlic, and salt together in a food processor until it forms a paste.

2. Add in the pumpkin puree, BBQ seasoning, cinnamon, and smoked paprika and pulse until well combined.

3. Top with pepitas, sprinkle of paprika, and swirl with your spoon to make it festive.

4. ENJOY!

HARVEST SALAD

This is one of those salads that should be made all year round. It should not be a recipe that is just kept for friends at Friendsgiving. Here's a thought: Why can't we celebrate Friendsgiving all year round? One of the best ways to build relationships is to share a meal with someone and verbalize your gratitude. Try having Friendsgiving in March—just to tell your friends thank you and that God has blessed your life with their friendship.

Prep: 10 min. | **Cook: 20 min.** | **Ready In: 30 min.** | **Serves: 10–12**

INGREDIENTS

1 14-ounce bag kale

Handful of candied pecans*

Handful of dried cranberries

Handful of pumpkin seeds

1–2 Honeycrisp apples, thinly sliced

½ cup crumbled feta cheese

APPLE CIDER VINAIGRETTE:

⅓ cup olive oil

1 shallot, diced

2 tablespoons balsamic vinegar

2 tablespoons apple cider vinegar

1 tablespoon fig preserves (the more the better)

1 tablespoon fresh thyme leaves

Kosher salt and pepper

Red pepper flakes (optional)

INSTRUCTIONS

1. In a large salad bowl, combine the kale, pecans, and cranberries.

2. To make the vinaigrette: Heat the ⅓ cup olive oil and balsamic vinegar in a medium skillet over high heat. When the oil shimmers, add the shallots. Cook until fragrant, 2–3 minutes. Remove from the heat and let cool slightly. Add the apple cider vinegar, fig preserves, and thyme. Season with salt and pepper, and you can add red pepper flakes for a nice kick.

3. Pour the vinaigrette over the salad, tossing to combine. The longer the dressing is on the salad, the more the kale will wilt and become softer and sweeter to eat!

4. Top the salad with pumpkin seeds, sliced apples, and feta. Eat and enjoy!

NOTE: If you love pears, you can slice pears very thinly and add them to the dressing as you are making it on the stove. This will marinate your pears and make them really soft! It will also give another texture to your salad—and I'm all about textures in salads!

CRANBERRY SALSA AND CREAM CHEESE

Christmas can be one of the busiest party seasons of the year but also the loneliest time of year if you attend the parties alone. We must consistently trust God because He uses these times to draw us closer to Him. So while you are making this salsa before the party, pray. Pray that God opens your eyes to His work in your life and the blessings of community He has brought you!

Prep: 5 min. | **Cook: 30 min.** | **Ready In: 35 min.** | **Serves: 12–14**

INGREDIENTS

1 12-ounce package fresh cranberries

½ cup granulated sugar

2 tablespoons orange juice

1 tablespoon lime juice

1 jalapeño pepper, deseeded and chopped

2 tablespoons chopped onion

¼ cup chopped fresh cilantro

1 8-ounce package cream cheese, softened

6 tablespoons sour cream

¼ teaspoon garlic powder

¼ teaspoon onion powder

1 tablespoon orange zest

Serve with crackers or sourdough toast

INSTRUCTIONS

1. Add cranberries and sugar to food processor and mix until coarsely chopped.

2. Stir in orange juice and lime juice then jalapeño, onion, and cilantro.

3. In a large mixing bowl, mix cream cheese, sour cream, garlic powder, and onion powder.

4. Put cream cheese mixture in bowl and top with cranberry mixture.

5. Top with orange zest and serve your guests for Christmas!

CHRISTMAS PUNCH

Prep: 5 min. | **Cook: 0 min.** | **Ready In: 5 min.** | **Serves: 10–12**

INGREDIENTS

24 ounces cranberry juice

12 ounces frozen orange juice concentrate

8 ounces apple cider

8 ounces ginger ale

1–2 oranges, for garnish

Fresh cranberries, for garnish

INSTRUCTIONS

1. Pour all four beverages into a bowl and stir to combine.

2. Garnish with orange zest, orange slices, and fresh cranberries.

PEPPERMINT BARK S'MORES

Little secret about me: I drink peppermint bark coffee with peppermint mocha creamer every morning, all year long, not just during December. Needless to say, this is my go-to dessert for any occasion. And it is a tasty one!

Prep: 10 min. | **Cook: 30 min.** | **Ready In: 40 min.** | **Serves: 10–12**

INGREDIENTS

½ cup unsalted butter, softened

½ cup light brown sugar

¼ cup granulated sugar

1 egg

2 teaspoons vanilla extract

1⅓ cups all-purpose flour

¾ cup graham cracker crumbs

1 teaspoon baking powder

¼ teaspoon salt

3 cups mini marshmallows

12 squares peppermint bark

1 cup peppermint crumbles

INSTRUCTIONS

1. Preheat oven to 350 degrees F and grease a 9x9 baking pan.

2. Add butter and both sugars to a bowl and beat until light and fluffy.

3. Add egg and vanilla until combined.

4. In a separate bowl mix flour, graham cracker crumbs, baking powder, and salt.

5. Combine with wet ingredients.

6. Place half the dough in the baking dish and bake for 15 minutes.

7. Remove from the oven and cover the bottom with the marshmallows, then layer the peppermint bark on top.

8. Dollop the remaining cookie dough mixture on top and sprinkle peppermint crumbles on top. Bake for another 15 minutes.

9. Allow the bars to cool completely before you cut into them.

NOTE: These are perfect for giving as a gift. Wrap in plastic wrap and add a big bow!

POMEGRANATE AND HORSERADISH FLATBREAD

"The LORD your God is in your midst, a mighty one who will save; he will rejoice over you with gladness; he will quiet you by his love; he will exult over you with loud singing" (Zephaniah 3:17 ESV). This verse perfectly exemplifies the kind of friend Jesus is and the kind of attributes we should strive for with friends. There's no better time than the holidays to have people over and expand your community! People are always looking for friends during the holidays. I'm not one for horseradish, but this creamy sauce totally makes this flatbread pop. It'll give your community something to talk about!

Prep: 10 min. | **Cook: 10 min.** | **Ready In: 20 min.** | **Serves: 6–8**

INGREDIENTS

HORSERADISH SAUCE:

1 cup horseradish

½ cup sour cream

½ cup mayonnaise

2 tablespoons freshly squeezed lemon juice

2 teaspoons salt

¼ teaspoon pepper

1 tablespoon Dijon mustard

2 teaspoons Worcestershire sauce

FLATBREAD:

2–3 slices naan bread

8 ounces Brie cheese, rind removed and sliced in ⅛-inch slices

½ cup fresh pomegranate arils

¼ cup brown sugar

2 sprigs fresh rosemary, finely chopped

INSTRUCTIONS

1. Mix all ingredients for horseradish sauce in a food processor until creamy.

2. Spread creamy sauce on naan. Top with Brie slices, then sprinkle on pomegranate and brown sugar and top with rosemary.

3. Bake for 9–11 minutes at 425 degrees F until cheese is browned and gooey.

ACKNOWLEDGMENTS

The dream of creating a cookbook has been mine for a while, but I had no idea what I wanted to put on each page. When God introduced me to the Table four years ago when I moved to Northwest Arkansas, I could not have imagined the journey He would take me on. Every word in this book is a small piece of a passion He has been developing in my heart over the last few years.

While God placed this passion on my heart, He used so many people to help make it happen.

To my family. For photographing, babysitting, reading and refining, praying, encouraging, and taste-testing all my recipes. You guys are just plain consistent, and I'm blown away by how you believe in all my crazy dreams. This book could not have come together without this tribe pushing me the entire way.

To my community. From doubt-filled late-night phone conversations to dinner parties full of encouragement—you showed up and believed in my message and this book. It's so true when they say behind every strong woman is a group of other strong women holding her up. Thank you for always being there.

To the powerhouse of people that helped bring this book to reality. Joy – for fighting for me from day one and pushing me to write this book. Gini, my faithful editor, for adopting this baby as your own and walking through each step of it with me. Becca – for bringing my vision to life with your amazing design. Jen and your team at Bradford Lit for prioritizing my message and supporting me throughout the process. Jason and Marc and the team behind you guys at DaySpring…I am blown away by your commitment to telling my story! And lastly, Molly Anne – shooting this book with a newborn baby, editing late into the night, and helping me bring every recipe to life, you are truly a gift.

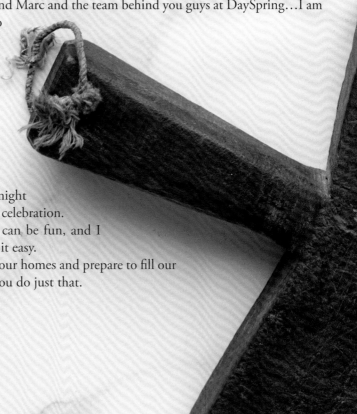

My prayer is that this book will empower every reader to have confidence in their hosting ability, no matter the moment. That moment could be a Tuesday night or a well-thought-out Friendsgiving celebration. Whatever the moment is, hosting can be fun, and I want to give you the tools to make it easy.

God is asking each of us to open our homes and prepare to fill our tables, and I pray this book helps you do just that.

To God be all the glory.

LIVE YOUR FAITH

Dear Friend,

This book was prayerfully crafted with you, the reader, in mind—every word, every sentence, every page—was thoughtfully written, designed, and packaged to encourage you...right where you are this very moment. At DaySpring, our vision is to see every person experience the life-changing message of God's love. So, as we worked through rough drafts, design changes, edits and details, we prayed for you to deeply experience His unfailing love, indescribable peace, and pure joy. It is our sincere hope that through these Truth-filled pages your heart will be blessed, knowing that God cares about you—your desires and disappointments, your challenges and dreams.

He knows. He cares. He loves you unconditionally.

BLESSINGS!
THE DAYSPRING BOOK TEAM

Additional copies of this book and
other DaySpring titles can be purchased
at fine retailers everywhere.
Order online at dayspring.com
or
by phone at 1-877-751-4347